Seeking the Pillar of FIRE

Uncovering God's Direction for a Local Church

Steven J. Musser and Eric A. Orke

Free Church Publications
Minneapolis, MN

Seek the Pillar of Fire

Published by Free Church Publications

Distributed by:
NextStep Resources
7840 12th Ave South
Minneapolis, MN 55425
www.nsresources.com
800-444-2665

ISBN 0-911802-93-2

Table of Contents

Preface

We believe that perhaps the greatest problem facing most local churches today is determining where God is leading them. Technology has revolutionized the way people live their lives and the values they hold. The world is growing smaller while the population grows larger and ever more diverse. Cultural values in the West have become increasingly secularized and faith is often defined individually under the umbrella of post-modernism.

Because of this, many local churches today find themselves in a position not unlike that of the Israelites during the Exodus. In an ever changing, ever more uncertain world they ask, "Where does God want us to go? How is He going to get us there, and who will He call to lead us?"

Most pastors and church leaders confess that they don't have a lot of confidence in their knowledge and understanding of how God leads a local church in today's context. As a result, they often wish God would provide them with a kind of "pillar of fire" like the biblical one He used to lead Israel out of Egypt, through the wilderness and into the Promised Land.

Yet despite the prevalence and critical importance of this perceived need, there is relatively little step-by-step practical help available to local churches who are seeking God's direction for them. Perhaps this is why, after much prayer, we felt God calling us to write this book.

The content of this book has been derived from our experience as pastors, as researchers and professors in the academic world, as church consultants, as district-level leaders in a large evangelical denomination and, most importantly, as men who have prayed earnestly for the local church. While most of what is written in this book is unique, it has been scrutinized and evaluated carefully to assure that it is aligned with the Scriptures and with the existing church knowledge base.

Seeking the Pillar of Fire

Our best advice on how to utilize the material in this book is for you to read the whole book in one or two sittings. Next, encourage your leadership team to read it and then spend some scheduled time discussing what you've read. As you will see, should you decide to implement the process described in this book into your church, the steps are carefully laid out and easy to follow.

We want to caution you, however, that the implementation of a process or formula will never yield God's direction for a local church. God alone leads each church. This is why the process laid out in this book requires the seeking of God's face at every step. Our experience has taught us that as you work through implementing the recommendations of this book, you will find them to be acts of godly devotion and not organizational techniques.

Our prayer is that this book might help your local church to enter into a new era of opportunity to grow God's kingdom and glorify our Lord. May God be with you.

Chapter 1
It's the Role of the Senior Pastor

One of the concerns we hear repeatedly from our pastors is the pressure they feel to be the "visionary leader" in the church. The way visionary leader is defined by them, and often defined in the church leadership literature, can be quite daunting. They are looked upon in many cases to provide a vision for the church that will increase attendance dramatically, draw young and talented families into the church, draw new leaders into the church, and draw new gifted givers into the church as well. We believe this not only breaks God's heart, it destroys the confidence of many God has called to the pastorate.

It's true that most of the people putting pressure on the pastor to be the visionary leader of the church poise their desire for vision as a desire for the kingdom to grow. But all too often, when really probed, they reveal that their true desire is for the pastor to either rescue the church from a serious decline or to take the church to the "next level" -whatever that means.

We find it amazing that this pressure on the pastor to be a visionary emanates from so many quarters of the church. It often comes from the congregation, from the church Board, from associate pastors, from denominational leaders and, particularly, from the church leadership literature.

For example, Aubrey Malphurs puts it this way:

> ...nonvisionary senior pastors and their churches will struggle with a general lack of clear direction. I have found that often nonvisionary leaders discover they function better and are happier in support positions rather than point positions. This is because people do not expect them to have a vision; whereas they do expect the senior person to have one. (Malphurs, 1999, p. 144)

He then suggests that pastors take the Myers-Briggs Type Indicator

(MBTI) or the Kiersey Temperment Sorter to discover if they have the prerequisite disposition to be visionary leaders. The response of many pastors to this kind of pressure and expectation is troubling and sometimes heart-breaking.

For example, not that long ago, one of the pastors in our district called me and asked if he could meet me for lunch. He said he had something important he wanted to talk over with me. This pastor was the pastor of a church of about 350 average Sunday attendance. He had been the senior pastor there for 13 years during which the church successfully completed a building expansion program and hired two other associate pastors. The church had grown under his leadership too – not exponentially, but steady growth nevertheless.

After we were finished with our sandwiches and the small talk banter that always takes place among pastors when they meet and eat together, his demeanor suddenly fell. I noticed that he was looking down and was trying to avoid eye contact with me. Then he said in a soft, small voice, "I think I might be stepping down from the pastorate of my church soon." I was stunned. I didn't expect this from him.

"Why?" I said. "Has another church called you?"

"No," he answered. "I have no place at all that I'm looking at right now. You see, I'm not simply considering leaving my church, I'm thinking about leaving the ministry."

Now I was really shocked. Immediately the wheels in my mind started turning. *Oh no*, I thought. *Don't tell me he's had a moral failure.*

He looked straight at me and said, "I guess you want to know why."

I said, "Yeah. This is a real shocker to me. I thought things were going so well. I even mentioned you in at a recent pastoral gathering and held up you and your church as a model. What happened?"

He said, "Well actually, it's been brewing for the last year or two. My board has lost confidence in me to lead."

Again I was astonished. "But why?" I asked. "You seem to have been doing so well."

"That's what I thought," he said. "But about 18 months ago my board chair suggested that we all read a book together about church leadership. We gave one meeting a month to the book as we discussed a few chapters at a time with each other. Then it happened. The board began probing me about my thoughts on the chapter on vision. Naively I said I thought that it was a good chapter but that I wasn't really a visionary pastor." Then he said, "I suddenly noticed that they were all just staring at me with a look of concern and disappointment."

He told me that his board chair asked to meet him for breakfast later in the week. At the breakfast his board chair said that they had had an informal meeting without him a few weeks earlier in which they all expressed concern that the church didn't seem to have the kind of clear direction and vision that a few of the surrounding churches seemed to have. He told him that they all felt that the church needed an empowering, stimulating vision because without it, they could see the churches around them siphoning off people from their congregation and hurting the viability of the church.

I asked, "How did you respond to him?"

"At first," he said, "I thought, okay…I can do this, I'll give it a try." He told me that he then began reading all he could on church vision and attended a number of church leadership conferences that focused on vision casting.

"What did you discover?" I asked. Again his face fell. He looked down and said, "I discovered that I can't do it. That I'm not a visionary and I never will be." He went on to say that he truly loved his church and that he deeply respected his board. He said, "I just think the church would be better off with some other guy – you know, a visionary guy who could lead the church to its full potential."

"But what about you?" I asked. "What are you going to do?"

He looked at me with eyes that were slowly becoming red around the edges and said, "You know, maybe my time has passed. Maybe the time has come when guys like me just aren't needed anymore. You read all the church leadership stuff; it's as if the church has gone on without me."

He then shared the agony he was going through. He related how clearly he had sensed God's call – how clearly he believed God had led him into the pastorate. But now, he wasn't so sure anymore. Perhaps he had misread or misunderstood God's call. Perhaps God had removed his calling. Perhaps God now had other things for him to do that didn't require him being a pastor.

All of this over "church vision." Is being a visionary leader really

9

that hard? Is it necessary to have an appropriate disposition to lead and grow a local church? Our conclusion is that it can't be this difficult. We certainly don't see this kind of visionary constraint on church leaders down through the centuries.

And yet, we are living in an age unlike any other with respect to the speed of change. Never before has history witnessed the accelerated rate of change that we are experiencing in the 21st century. Everything seems to be approaching light speed and the church too is impacted by this constant change. It always has been. The church today would be hardly recognizable in the first century, or in Medieval times, or in the Renaissance, or in the Reformation. God's truth will never change. The Gospel will never change. God's word will always be His word to us. But the way the church is governed, the way it relates to the world around it, the way it frames the hope of the Gospel will always have to change to meet the needs an ever changing world presents.

And this is why so many churches are "seeking the pillar of fire." This is why so many churches are focused on determining God's direction for them in this changing world through the process of vision casting. But surely this cannot mean that only pastors high on sensing (S) or intuiting (N) on the MBTI are being called to lead God's church in this age.

But there are additional fundamental problems with the notion that it is the senior pastor who must cast the church's vision – that it is the senior pastor alone who is responsible to seek the pillar of fire. If the senior pastor alone is expected to define the church's direction through vision casting, how can others in the church become confident that what they are hearing is truly from God? That is, how can they be sure that the vision the pastor is presenting and casting is a true reflection of God's direction for the church?

The unfortunate scenario in which the congregation and/or church leaders begin to question the pastor's vision is a common occurrence among evangelical churches. The congregation and church leaders often invest much of their lives in a local church. Many were often members of the church before their current pastor ever came to serve. As such, they have a unique sense of their local church's history, culture and experience and they have a vague, but often firm understanding of what they believe will and will not work in their local church.

The senior pastor, on the other hand, often comes to a local church with little to no understanding of its history, culture and experience. So when he is called upon to cast the vision for the future direction of the church, he often depends upon what he has learned about the visions of other churches he's visited or read about; upon the visions that are shared at church conferences the pastor attends; or, more likely, upon the pastor's sense of calling. Unfortunately, all three of these can lead to disagreement and conflict.

For example, one of the pastors in our district felt great pressure from his board to cast a vision for the future direction of their local church. His board was comprised of a number of very effective professionals in the secular world and the pressure on the pastor seemed almost palpable to him. As a response to this pressure, the pastor began praying and seeking God's direction for the church by reading every book on vision and the future of the church that he could get his hands on. He attended church leadership summits and church leadership development conferences. And like a dry sponge placed into a bucket of water began absorbing ideas and advice at an incredible pace.

Because of the plethora of church visions he had been exposed to, it took him almost two years to finally settle on one. As you might imagine, his board was growing increasingly impatient with his lack of ability to vision cast for their local church.

Finally, he decided and then shared a rather blended, homogenized vision with the board. Although they had a few concerns and expressed some tough questions to him, they believed it was the pastor's role alone to cast vision and determine the future of their local church, so they chose to support him and encouraged him to move forward.

Things were fine for the first few months. The pastor shared the vision with the congregation who responded with expected apathy after which he pressed ahead to meet with other church leaders to plan implementation. About three months into the planning stage the pastor just happened to have a conversation with another pastor in the district who very highly recommended a recently published book to him about the future direction of evangelical churches. He took his friend's advice, bought the book and read it in one weekend.

After reading the book, the pastor began to be filled with fresh excitement about what he had read. He also began questioning the quality and content of the vision he had just cast. He formulated some new ideas that incorporated what he had just learned from the book he read and met with his board. At the meeting he spent about an hour trying to encapsulate the book's message for them. He then proceeded to share what he believed was a far better vision for their church.

His board was taken aback by this new vision but after several more meetings they chose to stand behind the pastor and allow him to present the "new and improved" vision to the congregation. After all, the board believed to a person that it was the pastor's role and responsibility to determine vision and future direction for the church.

Once again, the pastor shared the vision with a largely apathetic congregation and began meeting with leaders to plan implementation. And then it happened again. The pastor attended a leadership summit about six months later and was very deeply moved by the visionary presentation of one of the speakers.

As you may have already guessed, he went back to his board still another time and once again tried to encapsulate what he had heard that moved him so deeply at the summit. He then presented still another vision. But this time the board was exasperated. His chair said, "We simply don't believe that this is how God leads His church. We simply don't believe that you are hearing from God. Not only are you continually changing the vision, you are recommending a future direction that many of us believe does not fit with the way God has formed and built this church. This just isn't how we believe God is leading this church." The pastor was disappointed, frustrated and somewhat angry that his board was not allowing him to lead. Six months later the board let him go.

Now this story may indeed be a bit extreme. Hopefully most pastors are not that capricious and uncertain when it comes to formulating vision. But it does raise an interesting issue. If people believe that vision is the responsibility of the pastor and, if the pastor isn't "visionary," then he is likely to search for help. In so doing, he is likely to look at what other respected church leaders are saying about the future of the evangelical church as a whole and then use this to try and formulate a vision for his church. The result is never knowing when to settle, when to change, when to revise. The church leadership literature is continually publishing and promoting visionary material for non-visionary pastors. How does the pastor choose? Most pastors in this kind of situation are in deep prayer asking God to show them – to help them choose. But many pastors report that they have struggled to hear God's response to them.

There is still another problem with the notion that it is the senior pastor's role and responsibility to seek the pillar of fire that causes people in the church to question whether the pastor's vision is really God's direction. This occurs when the pastor feels forced to resort to his particular calling to determine a local church's vision. In this scenario, which we have witnessed often, the pressure from the congregation and church leaders on the pastor to cast vision leads them to introspection. The pastor begins to reflect back on the kind of ministry he felt God was calling him to when he acknowledged God's call on his life. And it is this calling that becomes the vision.

One pastor in our district experienced this firsthand. He came to pastor a church with little to no knowledge of the church's history, culture and experience. When told by his board that they were expecting him to cast a new vision for the church, he relied upon his calling as he prayed for God's direction. While this pastor was a master communicator who could preach alongside perhaps the best, his calling was to reach the unlovely. He felt a particular call to reach drug addicts, prostitutes and the homeless with the hope found in Jesus.

The church he pastored also cared deeply for the lost. They had a history of effective outreach and many who were now attending the church had come to faith through the outreach and evangelism that took place through this church. But they were a professional church made up of many doctors, lawyers and business people. And while they had a heart for "all" of the lost, not just people like them, they nevertheless didn't feel particularly called to focus on drug addicts and prostitutes.

The clash was inevitable. At a congregational meeting where the pastor was sharing his deep passion for the unlovely and his certain belief that this was the vision God was calling the church to follow, a well-mannered and soft spoken senior rose to his feet and very gently said, "Pastor, I can tell you care very deeply about this vision and that God has indeed called you to this type of ministry. But how can we know that your vision is the vision God has for us?"

The pastor, who was very sensitive and aware, could only respond that he had been praying long and hard for God's leading. The older gentleman then carefully said, "I've been praying long and hard too. I wonder why God has allowed us to see things so differently." Six months later the pastor left and started a new church that embodied the vision that reflected God's ministry calling on his life. It has been very successful.

The second fundamental problem with the notion that it is the senior pastor's role and responsibility to cast vision and determine the future direction of a local church is one of ownership. The secular leadership world understands this issue perhaps better than the church. For it is a well-known principle in secular leadership writing and research that regardless of how exciting and stimulating a vision is, if people don't own it – it is destined to fail. That is, people can get very excited about "your" vision. But that doesn't mean that they'll commit themselves to fulfilling your vision. To do that, they have to own the vision personally. It has to be theirs. It has to be a part of them.

The sad reality is that in many churches that believe that it is the role and responsibility of the senior pastor to formulate and cast the vision, the congregation remains largely unmoved and unchanged. Some may agree with the pastor's vision and give public support to it at meetings, etc. But unless they own it personally, they will sacrifice little to see it become reality.

Later chapters will address this issue of ownership in much more detail. At this point, perhaps it is sufficient to simply point out that a pastor unilaterally "declaring" the vision does not mean people will own it personally even when the pastor argues forcefully that the vision is God's. Most believers are rightfully cautious to embrace something just because that person believes God has spoken it to them. This is true, even when there exists great respect for the vision caster. Wise believers are aware that the flesh is weak and that it should be a frightening thing to utter the words, "God has spoken to me on your behalf." Yet this is exactly what many churches force their pastors to do in seeking the pillar of fire.

Chapter 2
It's the Role of the Board

One of the fulfilling parts of serving in district leadership is meeting with church boards. It is always encouraging to see how seriously these volunteer leaders take their role. Many believe that God has placed them in leadership and they desire to serve him wholeheartedly with their gifts and abilities. They realize that, among other things, they have oversight of the doctrine, discipling and direction of their church. And church members know that as well; regularly contacting board members with recommendations and questions. And one of the questions most often asked is "Where is our church headed?"

As was discussed in the last chapter, many local churches expect the pastor to be the visionary leader and provide a clear and exciting direction. The expectations of the board are that the pastor will bring to them and then to the congregation a vision that will be exciting and transform the church. However, there are some church boards that have very different expectations. Many believe it is their responsibility, as spiritual leaders, to prayerfully and carefully develop the church vision. The pastor may be a part of the process of developing the vision; but not as the leader. Rather, he simply is seen as one among equals.

For example, a pastor was hired as the associate pastor of discipleship in a growing church in our district. During the interviews before he was hired he recognized that the board members were impressed that he had a business background before going to seminary. They felt his expertise would be helpful for him to fully understand the issues that church members encounter in the marketplace. In addition, they felt his organizational expertise would be a great help to the church. But he was still surprised when one day he found out that he would be leading a vision retreat at the end of his first month at the church. The church chair met with him two weeks before the retreat and told him how happy he was to have someone who understood the visioning and planning process. He was looking forward to the board going through a S.W.O.T. analysis (Strengths, Weaknesses, Opportunities and Threats) and using the results to formulate a compelling vision.

I asked the pastor, "How did the day go?"

"We started with a good time of prayer. It was so encouraging that each of the board members wanted the church to go forward in a powerful way. They really have good hearts."

"Was the S.W.O.T. analysis helpful?"

"Well, to an extent. It led to some interesting discussion but wasn't a big part of formulating the vision."

"If that's the case, how was the vision developed?'

The pastor thought for a moment and then said, "There are some sharp people on the board. They come from a variety of backgrounds and many have gone through visioning and planning processes in their workplaces. And this was a problem. We ended up spending a lot of time defining and redefining what we were doing. Some of the board members wanted to adapt what we were doing to build in elements of the vision process that they thought had been helpful in their respective workplaces. Once we agreed on our approach I realized that each of the board members had a ministry area in the church that was near and dear to them – or their spouse. They were very strong in their opinions as to why their interest area should be a major focus in the new vision."

I replied, "While it is always good to see people have a strong commitment to their ministry area, it can make it difficult to come to agreement in developing a vision. Was there anything else that impacted the process?"

"There was one thing. As you can imagine, the characteristics and backgrounds of the members came out. I learned a lot about our board in one day! Some were very strong personalities; some were very eloquent and persuasive; some were new to the church; some were with the church since it was planted 20 years ago; some were well read in church leadership; and so on. I think you get the idea. These are great people but even with spirited discussion we went in circles quite a bit."

"So how did the vision finally turn out?" I asked.

"To be honest, it wasn't sharp and focused because the differing personalities, backgrounds and perspectives led us to try to accommodate everyone. It ended up with nice sounding words but kind of bland. It wasn't very compelling."

This situation reveals many of the very real pitfalls associated with a group developing a vision. We all laugh at the well known saying that "a camel is a horse designed by a committee," but there are many elements of truth in those words. Because board members come with so many different abilities, gifts, priorities and interests, it is often difficult to fashion a sharp focused vision. In addition, stronger personalities may influence the process as more reserved members keep their ideas to themselves. As a matter of fact, just as some pastors do not feel that they are the visionary leaders, many board members also do not feel that they are visionary and are reluctant to contribute. As good as well known marketplace models may be for developing vision, we do not believe that they are transferable to discerning vision in the local church.

A board member from another church once shared that after their board developed their church's vision they set aside another day to come together to develop a plan to communicate it to the congregation. "Quite frankly," he said, "the board carefully thought through a variety of ways to share the vision. Unfortunately, what we ended up doing was to develop a way to "sell" the vision to the congregation." He said this was because the board felt that although they were unified in the vision they developed, they knew there would be several pockets of resistance in the church. So the board talked about sending letters, holding meetings, delivering sermons and visiting classes and small groups to explain their thinking.

I asked him, "How did it go?"

"We all knew the importance of developing an effective communication strategy to communicate the vision," he answered. "That was a given. But to be honest, it felt a little odd trying to convince people to get behind a vision in which they had no input. Ours is a gracious congregation and we didn't get any heavy pushback but we also didn't get the wholehearted endorsement we hoped for either."

This situation points out the vital importance of the ownership of the vision throughout the congregation. Having the church board develop the vision, no matter how well it is communicated, does not guarantee ownership. True ownership occurs when as many church members as possible have input into it. Again, as stated earlier, the issue of ownership will be carefully dealt with in later chapters.

It is our belief that church boards are not the ones to develop the vision. Some board members may take issue with this, saying that it is their Biblical role as leaders to provide the direction for their church. They would argue that even if there are potential problems with the process as described above, with prayer and concern for each other's viewpoints, vision can be developed and communicated successfully.

We believe the board does indeed have a vital role in the vision process because the board is ultimately responsible for the direction of the church. However, in Chapter Four we will clearly show, through an examination of Scripture, how that role can be better understood.

Chapter 3
It's the Domain of God

Determining the direction of an organization in the secular world and uncovering direction for the church are two entirely different things. In the secular world, the leader (President, CEO, Executive Director, etc.) is called upon to engage in a process of creative, innovative thinking in which he or she "creates" a vision for the organization. In this process, the secular leader is encouraged to reflect deeply on the organization and its environment and to think "outside the box." That is, the vision of a leader in the secular world is first, the product of an objective analysis of the organization and its environment; and second, the outflow of the leader's personal passions and creative insights.

Not so the church. We believe church leaders must avoid at all costs the use of the secular model in discovering a church's vision. For ultimately, as will be discussed later in this chapter, it is God's vision that must be uncovered; it is God's vision that must be discerned. A church's vision must never come from a leader's creative insights or from thinking outside the box. Indeed, most Christians don't and shouldn't care about their pastor's personal vision for their church. Nor should they care about their board's vision for their church. They want to know God's vision for their church.

Unfortunately, much of the Christian leadership literature has tried to merge and integrate visioning in the secular world with visioning in the church. Often the church leader is encouraged to use the same principles and techniques that the secular world uses when developing vision – but with one key difference. The Christian leader is to bathe his efforts in prayer. It is this "bathing in prayer" that is meant to ensure that the final product will reflect the will of God and not the mind of the church leader.

The problem with this, as was alluded to in the first two chapters, is that people in the congregation are reduced to simply taking the word of the pastor or board that they clearly have heard from God and have uncovered His vision for their church. This is why so many times when the vision is rolled out to a congregation by church leaders they begin with phrases like, "After much prayer, we have come to believe..." or "After praying fervently for God's direction, we believe..." The problem, of course, occurs when others in the congregation, who have also been seeking God's face in prayer concerning the future direction of the church, come to a different understanding of His vision for them.

When this happens confusion often erupts. Congregants and leaders are forced to decide who has and who has not really been hearing from God. God is not a God of disorder but of peace in the church (I Cor. 14:33). Therefore the only reasonable conclusion that can be drawn when, despite fervent prayer by all, leaders and congregants arrive at different conclusions regarding their church's future direction is that one of them must not truly have heard from God. One of them must be deceived. The question, of course, is which one. Who got it wrong? Which of them only "thinks" they have heard from God and which of them really has?

Under circumstances like this, power and authority often determine the outcome. Those in church leadership positions rightfully expect their discernment to be evaluated deferentially because of their position. And congregants with opposing conclusions often do remain silent, not wishing to violate the biblical mandates to obey their leaders (e.g. Hebrews 13:17).

It can be argued, of course, that the biblical mandates for church congregants to obey their leaders most often refer to matters of church order, of the interpretation and application of doctrine and of church discipline. Nevertheless, many congregants suppress their opposing sense of discernment regarding the direction of their church in order to comply with what they see as a clear call to obey their leaders.

However, just because congregants may suppress their opposing sense of discernment, this does not mean that they will therefore passionately embrace the vision their leaders unilaterally uncovered instead. Many congregants simply assume a passive posture and sit back to wait for the leaders' vision to be confirmed over time. Unfortunately, it is this "wait and see" behavior that almost guarantees the leaders' vision will not be effective.

It seems both practical and prudent that the congregation have at least some role in the visioning process if meaningful ownership is to take place. But suggesting that the congregation has a role to play in a church's visioning process does not mean that the church's vision should then become the product of the congregation's collective insight or creativity.

Clearly, uncovering and discerning God's vision for a church must involve both leaders and congregants in a joint process if it is to be effective. But this process MUST avoid the temptation to generate a vision. Church visioning is always *a process of uncovering* God's direction and *never a process of creation* as it is in the secular world.

For since the inception of the church, it has always been God who has led and directed His people like He did the Israelites when they left Egypt. But perhaps the greatest example of God leading and guiding His people after the resurrection and ascension of Jesus is found in Acts chapter 10.

Becoming a child of God always has been a matter of faith and nothing else. That was true in the Old Testament and it is true in the New Testament. But before Acts 10, the best expression of saving faith was to worship God in His Temple in Jerusalem and to live and behave as a Jew. Gentiles couldn't come to Him as they were. If God had not written Acts chapter 10 into history the only way Gentiles could become full-fledged children of God would have been to follow the example of Ruth the Moabitess when she told Naomi, "Your people will be my people and your God, my God."

But then a most wonderful thing happened. God wrote Acts 10 into history and in so doing He revealed an astounding new vision for His newly founded church. He gave Gentiles the opportunity to become full-fledged children of God through nothing more than faith in His Son. No longer did they have to give up their identity and live and behave like a Jew to be His children. No, all they had to do now was to believe with all of their hearts that Jesus was who He said He was – the Holy, incarnate Son of God – and that He did what the Bible says He did – that He died in our place on the cross for the forgiveness of sins.

If the Jewish believers in the early church had tried to cast this vision on their own it would have undoubtedly resulted in a costly and dismal failure. The Jewish believers in the early church likely would have been very suspicious of the Council at Jerusalem if they simply told them that after much prayer, they had come to the conclusion that God now was leading them to throw open the door of the church and hence the door of salvation to any Gentile throughout the world on the basis of faith and faith alone.

The new vision for the church, which totally opened it to Gentile believers and that gave them full equality with Jews, was a radical new vision for God's people. Early believers certainly would have wanted evidence that this radical new direction for God's people was truly from God and not from a vision casting retreat held by the Council at Jerusalem.

I believe this is why God delivered His vision to the early church the way He did. He let down a sheet from heaven with unclean animals in it and then ordered, "Get up, Peter. Kill and eat." To which Peter replied, "Surely not Lord! I have never eaten anything impure or unclean." The voice spoke to him a second time, "Do not call anything impure that God has made clean." This happened three times, and immediately the sheet was taken back to heaven. (Acts 10: 11 – 16)

Acts 10 continues with accounts of two miracles meant to convince the early church that this new vision was indeed from God and not from man. First, just after the sheet was taken back up to heaven, people from Cornelius, a Roman centurion, arrived at the house where Peter was staying. The Spirit then spoke to Peter and told him to welcome these Gentiles because they were sent by God. The Gentiles shared with him that a holy angel told Cornelius to have Peter come to him so that he could hear what he had to say.

Second, when Peter arrived, Cornelius told him how a man in shining clothes had spoken to him and had told him to send for Peter. At this Peter declares, "I now realize how true it is that God does not show favoritism but accepts men from every nation who fear Him and do what is right." (Acts 10: 34 - 35) After he shared the gospel with them Peter noticed how the Holy Spirit had come on all those who had heard the message and that they were speaking in tongues and praising God. He then said, "Can anyone keep these people from being baptized with water? They have received the Holy Spirit just as we have." (Acts 10:47)

In Acts 11, Peter then goes to the Council at Jerusalem and relates all that had happened. That is, he related his personal encounter with God on the rooftop when the sheet was lowered; he related how an angel had spoken to the Gentile Cornelius and how he was called to share the gospel with all of Cornelius' household; and, he related how once the Gentiles there heard the message of salvation, they began praising God and speaking in tongues. After hearing of Peter's encounter the Council raised no further objections and praised God saying "So then, God has granted even the Gentiles repentance unto life." (Acts 11:18)

Now the rest of the book of Acts indicates that God's vision for including all believing Gentiles into the church remained highly controversial. But God's direction for the church had been discerned, His vision had been cast; and the world was never the same.

But what are we to draw from this example that might be useful to a body of believers seeking God's direction for their local church? First, it was clear that it was God Himself who did the leading. God Himself generated the vision, not church leaders. Second, a significant leader in the church (in this case Peter) had a personal encounter with God in which the vision was revealed. The importance of this will be addressed more completely in chapter 5 and how it actually takes place will be discussed in chapters 8 and 9. Third, the leader who had encountered God shared his experience with the leadership of the church (in this case the Council at Jerusalem) for them to test it against the Scriptures. And fourth, the church leaders then shared the vision with the church as a whole and sought to implement it as they sent out Paul and others.

It is certainly fair to question whether this very significant moving of God in directing His entire church should be used as a model for seeking God's direction for a particular local church. Our best response to this question is simply that we have seen God accomplish this over and over again in many local churches. There will be detailed discussions of these examples in chapters 8 through 10 that will support this notion more strongly.

But at this point, it is simply our desire to stress and reiterate that a local church's vision for their future must come from God Himself – not from a rational decision-making process among church leaders. The notion that God actually gives local churches distinctive visions to direct their future is the subject matter of the next chapter.

Chapter 4
A Church's Spiritual DNA

Every now and then we get a request from a church to facilitate a retreat at which the church's leaders will seek to revise or update their church's mission. Our immediate response to them is "But you can't do that!" When they ask why not, we tell them that the mission of every church has already been prescribed by Jesus and it's not available for revision.

At this point they usually look at us with a confused look. We then explain to them that their confusion is likely a problem of semantics. The terms mission and vision are defined quite differently in the church leadership literature and sometimes used interchangeably. Since there is no right or wrong definition of these terms, it will be helpful to offer our definition and use of them.

We define mission simply as the purpose for which the church exists. Although there are a variety of ways in which it can be described, we believe that ultimately the mission of the church must be some combination of "to fulfill the Great Commission" (i.e. to spread the Gospel from Jerusalem, to Judea, to Samaria and to the ends of the earth – Matthew 28: 19; Acts 1: 8) and, "to teach believers to obey Christ's commands" (i.e. to help them become more like Jesus – Matthew 28: 20; I John 2:6).The Scriptures seem to make it very clear. The purpose or mission of every church is ultimately the same. And since this purpose has been defined and established by God, it is not up for periodic revision at weekend leadership retreats.

Of course, most often when church leaders ask us to lead a "mission revision retreat," they are really asking us to lead a "vision revision retreat." Once again, it is the definition of terms that makes the difference.

Our definition of a local church's vision is "the distinctive contribution that God desires your church to make to the mosaic of churches that make up the church universal." Thus, while every church has the same mission (to help people fulfill the great commission and to help them obey the great commandments), the visions God desires to impart to them may be quite distinct from one another.

Why would God desire to impart a variety of visions among His local churches? Well first, it's His nature to express His majesty in diversity.

One of my favorite television programs has been a documentary series titled, "The Universe." It may be produced by godless, secular humanists, but I love it anyway. In fact, many of the episodes have become deeply worshipful experiences for me. As I watch, I contemplate the diversity of God's creative power in the existence of pulsars, quasars, black holes and the billions and billions of galaxies each with billions and billions of stars in them.

As I contemplate all of this, I am often emotionally and spiritually overwhelmed by the awesome power and majesty of God. And then I consider the unthinkable – that this awesome creator God is the same God who loves "me." He is the same God who numbers the hairs on my head. He is the same God that knew me before I was ever conceived, who ordained all my days before any of them came to pass. And He is the same God who sent His precious Son to die in my place to atone for my sins.

As I ponder the greatness and power of God in His creation I find myself humbled and sometimes breathless. Tears run down my cheeks as I realize that everything we see, everything we know was created by Him and through Him – the stars, the planets, the earth, the mountains, the oceans, the plant life, the fish, the birds, the animals – ALL OF IT – was simply spoken into existence at the command of His voice.

The God of creation delights our eyes with the beauty of sunshine and deep blue skies dotted with puffs of pure white clouds. He delights our eyes with the hues of sunsets and with the myriad of colors of beautiful flowers in the Spring. He delights our eyes with a fantastic tapestry of color as the leaves change in the Fall. And He delights our eyes with the beauty of the sparkling white snow that blankets the earth in Winter.

He delights our tongues with the exquisite taste of luscious fruit and foods of all kinds. He delights our ears with the music of songbirds and the call of creatures and with the gifts of songwriters and musicians.

He delights our noses with the sweet scents of lilacs and honeysuckle – with the fresh smelling air after a newly fallen rain. He delights our touch with the softness of a lamb and with the texture of a leaf.

He delights our imagination with how He takes tiny atoms of matter and delicately interweaves them into the pattern of a double helix to form DNA as He breathes life into these molecules and creates each of us in His image. God delights our hearts with the cry of a newborn baby, each one different, each one unique.

You see, truly it is God's nature to express His majesty in diversity. So instead of asking why God would desire to impart different visions to the local churches that comprise the Bride of Christ, perhaps the better question is, "Why wouldn't He do so?"

The second reason that God desires to impart a variety of visions to His local churches is because God is a planner. God's plans are complex and they stretch through the ages. On the first page of the scriptures in Genesis chapter one, it is clear that God had a plan for the development of everything. Each day God precisely created exactly what He wanted and then on the seventh day He took a day of rest. Later in the Old Testament, in the Book of Joshua, First and Second Samuel and First and Second Kings, we find examples of numerous plans that were inspired by God. One of the most interesting plans can be seen in the Book of Nehemiah. Under the leadership of the Spirit, Nehemiah developed a plan for rebuilding the walls of Jerusalem. Esther also had a plan, Naomi had a plan, Nathan had a plan, Elijah had a plan and David had many plans. And all of these plans came into being through the inspiration of God's Spirit.

In the New Testament, we find that Jesus had a plan in sending out the disciples two by two. He told them what they could expect and what to do if things didn't work out. Of course, one of the greatest of Jesus' plans is found in Matthew. We call it the Great Commission. In it, Jesus gave a comprehensive plan that is for all Christians.

Of course, the greatest plan of all in the Bible, the plan that overarches all others, is God's plan for redeeming humankind. From the very beginning, the Bible says that God had a plan to redeem His creation. This plan will continue until the return of Jesus.

In Acts 1:8, when Jesus gave His final commands to His disciples, He clearly gave them a plan. As discussed earlier, He told them to begin evangelizing Jerusalem and then Judea, Samaria and eventually the ends of the earth.

Thus, the fact that God demonstrates His majesty in diversity and that He engages in complex and ongoing planning seems to provide a solid rationale for why God would desire to impart a variety of visions to the local churches that comprise His one true church. But if this is the case, is there any evidence of this diversity of visions in the Scriptures?

Consider the vision/spiritual DNA of the church at Berea.

> Now the Bereans were of more noble character than the Thessalonians, for they received the message with great eagerness and examined the Scriptures every day to see if what Paul said was true. (Acts 17:11)

Clearly this New Testament church had a passion for truth and a high view of the Scriptures. They had a God-given vision of being "noble in character" which wisely led them to test everything with the Scriptures, even the teachings of Paul.

Then there was the church at Ephesus.

> I know your deeds, your hard work and your perseverance. I know that you cannot tolerate wicked men, that you have tested those who claim to be apostles but are not, and have found them false. You have persevered and have endured hardships for my name, and have not grown weary. (Rev. 2: 2 – 3)

This New Testament church had a God-given vision for enduring suffering for the cause of Christ.

Consider also the churches of Macedonia.

> And now, brothers, we want you to know about the grace that God has given the Macedonian churches. Out of the most severe trial, their overflowing joy and their extreme poverty welled up in rich generosity. For I testify that they gave as much as they were able, and even beyond their ability. Entirely on their own, they urgently pleaded with us for the privilege of sharing in this service to the saints. And they did not do as we expected, but they gave themselves

first to the Lord and then to us in keeping with God's will. (2 Corinthians 8: 1 – 5)

Their God-given vision was to be an example of generosity to other local churches, even today's local churches. Their example of deeply sacrificial giving in the midst of their poverty and their willingness to plead for the opportunity to give distinguishes them.

But are there any examples of God-given visions among local churches today? Well, one example is Sherwood Baptist Church in Albany, Georgia. This church is known by many for the three full-length feature movies they have produced. They include Flywheel, Facing the Giants and Fireproof. Their Senior Pastor Michael Catt says that thousands have come to Christ through these films as they've been shown around the world.

Here are some excerpts from a recent article about Sherwood Baptist Church in Christianity Today that was written by Peter Chattaway:

> For several years the members of Sherwood Baptist Church have had a vision: "To touch the world from Albany, Georgia." And thanks to the power of mass media, this church of about 3,000 members—located in a city of only 80,000 or so—has been able to do just that. Through its media ministry, the church has already produced two feature-length films with an all-volunteer cast and a mostly-volunteer crew. Given their incredibly low budgets, both films—especially Facing the Giants—have been enormously successful, in theaters and on DVD. Both films have also been distributed to over 50 countries around the world in a dozen subtitled languages. Now the church is putting the finishing touches on its third film, Fireproof, which opens on September 26, 2008. This time the folks at Sherwood are working with a budget of $500,000—still peanuts by Hollywood standards, but five times the budget of Giants—and they even have a professional Hollywood actor, Kirk Cameron of Growing Pains and Left Behind fame, in the lead role as a firefighter whose marriage is in trouble.
>
> But one thing has remained constant: the church's commitment to treating movies as ministry, rather than just a safe

form of entertainment.

..And what would the folks at Sherwood say to someone who was thinking of starting a movie-making ministry at their own church? "Make sure it's what God wants you to do," says Stephen. "We've told people, just because our church made a movie and it worked, it doesn't mean God's calling you to make a movie," he says. "One of the worst things that could happen is if every church out there tries to make a movie. If God hasn't called them to do that, they're going to be spinning their wheels." (Christianity Today, September/October 2008, Vol. 46, No. 5, page 14)

At the time this book was written, "Fireproof" had been released for several months and was an even greater success than Sherwood Baptist's previous two films. But we believe the most important thing we can learn from this excerpt from Chattaway's article are the telling words that came at the end by the gentlemen named Stephen. Stephen gets it when he says, "Just because our church made a movie and it worked, it doesn't mean God's calling you to make a movie." Stephen seems to understand the primary purpose of this chapter – to show that God desires to release a variety of visions into the local churches that comprise the Bride of Christ.

We believe that God has created a wonderful mosaic of church visions that He desires to impart to His churches; visions that will certainly transform the world as they are fulfilled. But how does God communicate these visions? This is what will be explored in chapter 5.

Chapter 5
God's Sovereign Revelation of His Vision

Most church leadership teams that we have worked with have a strong desire to lead effectively and to serve the Lord and their congregation well. However, they often grapple with two questions when it comes to establishing the direction for their church. First, where does the vision come from? Is the intuition and creativity of the leaders involved? Or does it come exclusively from God? And, second, if it comes exclusively from God, to whom does God reveal it? The church leadership team? The congregation? The pastor? The lack of clarity in dealing with these questions has the potential to lead to confusion and frustration.

We discussed the first of these questions in Chapter 3. We believe that church leaders must avoid the secular model in discovering their vision. It is not a vision that comes from creative insights or thinking outside the box. It is God's vision that must be discerned; His vision for their church. We firmly believe that God gives local churches distinctive visions to direct their futures and we will discuss how we believe local churches can uncover His vision for them in the latter chapters of this book.

The second question is answered throughout the pages of Scripture where there appears to be a pattern to whom God reveals His vision. It is not given to groups such as the leaders of tribes or nations or councils. Rather, His vision is given to an individual leader. Then, as part of the pattern, the individual leaders brings the vision they have received from God to their leadership teams to confirm it, and together work to implement it.

Moses, one of the most renowned leaders throughout history, was in the wilderness when God revealed His vision to him.

The Lord said, "I have seen the misery of my people in Egypt. I have heard them crying out because of their slave drivers, and I am concerned about their suffering. So I have come down to rescue them from the hand of the Egyptians and to bring them up out of that land into a good and spacious land, a land flowing with milk and honey – the home of the Canaanites, Hittites, Amorites, Perizzites, Hivites and Jebusites. And now the cry of the Israelites has reached me, and I have seen the way the Egyptians are oppressing them. So now, go. I am sending you to Pharaoh to bring my people, the Israelites out of Egypt." (Exodus 2:7-10)

After receiving this vision from God, Moses was instructed by God to meet with the elders of Israel.

"Go, assemble the elders of Israel and say to them, 'The Lord, the God of your fathers – the God of Abraham, Isaac and Jacob – appeared to me and said: I have watched over you and have seen what has been done to you in Egypt. And I have promised to bring you up out of your misery in Egypt into the land of the Canaanites, Hittites, Amorites, Perizzites, Hivites and Jebusites – a land flowing with milk and honey.'

"The elders of Israel will listen to you. Then you and the elders are to go to the King of Egypt and say to him…" (Exodus 3:16 – 18a)

The pattern was established. Moses received the vision from God. It was God's vision and not something Moses had created. He was told to bring the vision to the elders of Israel and they would listen to it. The elders were not to vote whether to accept it because it was a message given to Moses from the Lord. Then Moses and the elders were instructed to work together to bring it about.

This same pattern is clear when we look at the life and leadership of Nehemiah. During the Jewish exile he lived in Babylon and held the important and responsible position as cupbearer to King Artaxerxes. From his brothers he heard about the difficult conditions in Jerusalem and responded by mourning, praying and fasting for a number of days. Then Nehemiah took the bold step to ask the King to allow him to return to his own country to repair the walls of Jerusalem. This was not a decision that Nehemiah came to on his own – he did not create it - it was a vision that the Lord gave him.

> I went to Jerusalem, and after staying there three days I set out during the night with a few good men. I had not told anyone what my God had put in my heart to do for Jerusalem... (Nehemiah 2: 11-12a)

.   Nehemiah approached the King for permission, traveled to Jerusalem, and inspected the walls not because he, personally, thought it was a good idea. Rather he did all of this because God had put on his heart what he was to do.

After Nehemiah examined the walls, Nehemiah 2: 16 – 18b goes on to describe how he then brought his vision to the officials in Jerusalem.

> The officials did not know where I had gone or what I was doing, because as yet I had said nothing to the Jews or priests or nobles or official or any others who would be doing the work. Then I said to them, "you see the trouble we are in: Jerusalem lies in ruins, and its gates have been burned with fire. Come let us rebuild the wall of Jerusalem, and we will no longer be in disgrace." I also told them about the gracious hand of God upon me and what the king had said to me.

The leaders received the vision from Nehemiah and immediately began to implement it. "They replied, 'Let us start rebuilding.' So they began this good work." (Nehemiah 2: 18b). And the tremendous rebuilding project was completed in 52 days.

This same pattern of the leader receiving the vision from God, the elders accepting it as such and then following through with implementation is also evident in the New Testament. In Acts 10 Peter received, through the sheet vision, God's message that all believing Gentiles were included in the church. Chapter 3 carefully discussed the encounter that Peter had with God, but the point to be emphasized here is that this vision came to an individual leader. It did not come to the elders as a group.

Peter then traveled to Jerusalem and shared the vision with concerned apostles and brothers. After Peter's full explanation to them, Acts 11: 18 says: "When they heard this they had no further objections and praised God, saying, "So then, God has granted even the Gentiles repentance unto life.'" The council understood that it was God's vision for the direction of the church that Peter had received.

Another example comes from Paul and Barnabas. They accepted the vision that Peter had received from the Lord that believing Gentiles were to be part of the church. But as Acts 15: 1-2 describes not all people in the early church did.

> Some men came down from Judea to Antioch and were teaching the brothers:

> "Unless you are circumcised, according to the custom taught by Moses, you cannot be saved." This brought Paul and Barnabas into sharp dispute and debate with them. So Paul and Barnabas were appointed, along with some other believers to go up to Jerusalem to see the apostles and elders about this question.

It was clear that this was a critical time in the life of the young church. Among the believers there were still very different ideas of how a person came to faith. Some felt that individuals needed to be circumcised and believe the Law of Moses before a relationship with Christ could be theirs. The Council at Jerusalem convened to address this crucial issue. Peter was there and reaffirmed to the Council that God "made no distinction between us and them, for he purified their hearts by faith. Now then, why do you try to test God by putting on the necks of the disciples a yoke that neither we nor our fathers have been able to bear? No! We believe it is through the grace of our Lord Jesus that we are saved, just as they are." Acts 15: 9-11.

Paul, who was called by God to minister the riches of Christ to the Gentiles, then spoke to the Council. Acts 15:12 records that Barnabas joined him in speaking and "The whole assembly became silent as they listened to Barnabas and Paul telling about the miraculous signs and wonders God had done among the Gentiles through them." The elders, led by James, listened and tested the message against Scripture (Amos 9: 11-12). Then James stated: "It is my judgment, therefore, that we should not make it difficult for the Gentiles who are turning to God." (Acts 15:19) Then the Council followed through by sending a letter to Gentile believers expressing their position.

Like Peter before them, Paul and Barnabas shared with the Council what God had taught and shown them. The Council listened and accepted their position after testing it against the Word of God.

It is important that local churches today recognize and apply the Scriptural pattern laid out in this chapter. It will answer the "how" and "who" questions regarding vision. First, the "how." The vision for their church is not something that they develop or create but it comes from God. It is His vision for their particular church family. Second, the "who." As was seen in both the Old and New Testaments, the vision was given in each instance to one individual. It is then presented to the elders for their review, discussion and testing against Scripture. And, finally, all the elders take the lead in ensuring that the vision is implemented.

Chapter 6
Vision and the Priesthood of All Believers

In the last chapter we described the pattern of how God reveals His vision to one leader and that leader brings the vision to the rest of the church board. The board then joins with the leader to communicate and implement the vision. Some readers may be troubled with this pattern. Their concerns may be expressed in various ways by different groups in the church.

"Wait a minute," says the church board. "We believe strongly in the plurality of leaders working together to shape the future. We were placed on the board to serve God and our congregation and we spend much time before God in prayer seeking his wisdom.

"Wait a minute," exclaims the staff. "We feel like we have just lost our opportunity to provide our insights and expertise into the direction of the church. God reveals himself to us as well!"

"Wait a minute," comes from church members. "We are taught regularly that 'every member is a minister.' Signs with that saying are hung on the walls to remind us. If it is true that we are all ministers then we feel like we have lost our voice when we don't have any part in discovering the vision."

The question is: "Do the leaders, staff, and church members have a case? Are their concerns legitimate?" We will look to Scripture to answer these concerns as we continue to develop the model for uncovering God's direction for the local church.

Scripture states that all believers are a priesthood. First Peter 2: 4-5 says "As you come to him, the living Stone – rejected by men but chosen by God and precious to him – you also, like living stones, are being built into a spiritual house to be a holy priesthood, offering spiritual sacrifices acceptable to God through Jesus Christ." And verse 9 of the same chapter reads, "But you are a chosen people, a royal priesthood, a holy nation, a people belonging to God, that you may declare the praises of him who called you out of darkness into his wonderful light."

In the Old Testament priests were the mediators between the people and God; the Israelites had to go through them to God. They offered sacrifices to cover people's sins. Christ's work on the cross changed all that. He was the perfect sacrifice; the only sacrifice needed. Now every person can go directly to God through our mediator Jesus Christ; the High Priest.

1 Timothy 2: 5 says "for there is one God and one Mediator between God and men, the man Jesus Christ." And Hebrews 4: 14 -16 states "Therefore, since we have a great high priest who has gone through the heavens, Jesus the Son of God, let us hold firmly to the faith we profess. For we do not have a high priest who is unable to sympathize with our weaknesses, but we have one who has been tempted in every way just as we are – yet was without sin. Let us then approach the throne of grace with confidence, so that we may receive mercy and find grace to help us in our time of need."

We go directly to God through Jesus. A human priest is not necessary. We can confess our sins and know that we will receive forgiveness. We can approach God with a combination of humility and confidence and seek His will and direction for our lives. We can bring the needs of the world and the smallest need in our personal life before Him. We can ask for wisdom for our own lives as well as for our church. We can each have an intimate relationship with the God of the universe.

However, we are not to be Lone Ranger Christians. We do not live out our faith alone in this world. We are part of the church. We belong to one another. We serve together and Peter describes our interconnectedness as a temple. All the stones (the people) are essential and are interrelated. Again, 1 Peter 2: 5 states: "You also, like living stones, are being built into a spiritual house to be a holy priesthood, offering spiritual sacrifices acceptable to God through Jesus Christ." Christ is the cornerstone and we are all the living stones where, together, we are to offer spiritual sacrifices.

The Apostle Paul uses the metaphor of the Body of which Christ is the head. Ephesians 2: 22-23 says: "And God placed all things under his feet and appointed him to be head over everything for the church, which is his body, the fullness of him who fills everything in every way." Colossians 1:18 reads "And he is the head of the body, the church; he is the beginning and the firstborn from the dead, so that in everything he might have supremacy."

As members of the church, the body, we all receive spiritual gifts. "Each one should use whatever gift he has received to serve others, faithfully administering God's grace in its various forms." (1 Peter 4: 10)

Romans 12: 4-8 further describes the role each person has as a member of the body.

> Just as each of us has one body with many members, and these members do not have the same function, so in Christ we who are many form one body, and each member belongs to all the others. We have different gifts according to the grace given us. If a man's gift is prophesying, let him use it in proportion to his faith. If it is teaching, let him teach; if it is encouraging, let him encourage; if it is contributing to the needs of others, let him give generously; if it is leadership, let him govern diligently; if it is showing mercy, let him do it cheerfully. (Other discussions of the gifts of the body are in 1 Corinthians 12 and 1 Peter 4.)

In the church each gift is important and needed. Each member is vital to the life of the church and is to be treated with respect. Paul in 1 Corinthians 12: 14 – 26 uses the human body to teach this spiritual truth.

> Now the body is not made up of one part but of many. If the foot should say, "Because I am not a hand, I do not belong to the body," it would not for that reason cease to be part of the body. And if the ear should say, "Because I am not an eye, I do not belong to the body," it would not for that reason cease to be part of the body. If the whole body were an eye, where would the sense of hearing be? If the whole body were an ear, where would the sense of smell be? But in fact God has arranged the parts in the body, every one of them, just as he wanted them to be. If they were all one part, where would the body be? As it is, there are many parts, but one body.

The eye cannot say to the hand, "I don't need you!" And the head cannot say to the feet, "I don't need you!" On the contrary, those parts of the body that seem to be weaker are indispensable, and the parts that we think are less honorable we treat with special honor. And the parts that are unpresentable are treated with special modesty, while our presentable parts need no special treatment. But God has combined the members of the body and has given greater honor to the parts that lacked it, so that there should be no division in the body, but that its parts should have equal concern for each other. If one part suffers, every part suffers with it; if one part is honored, every part rejoices with it.

It is exciting to see a local church fulfill the Great Commission and the Great Commandment. It is a place where members come to the Lord and pray faithfully for their church. It is a place where individuals graciously and in unity serve in their giftedness - a place where, in fact, every member is a minister. It is a place where men and women gifted in leadership step up and lead. It is a place where the members desire to hear their Lord say "Well done, good and faithful servant."

So we go back to the concerns brought up at the beginning of the chapter. How can it be that only one person hears from God with God's vision for the church while, at the same time, all the members can seek God's will and purpose directly and are all called to serve? In examining Scripture, we have seen that both are true. In the coming chapters we will offer a way to bring these together in the life of the church.

Chapter 7
It All Begins with the Leaders' Motives

We believe the most critical factor in Christian leadership today is the leader's motive for leading. So it should come as no surprise that we also believe that the foundational requirement for a local church to enter into a process of seeking to uncover God's vision for them is a proper set of motives in that church's leaders.

Scripture clearly indicates that God wants the motives of His leaders to reflect a focus on others – to reflect a selfless motive emerging from deep humility. Indeed, it seems that the only leaders God bestowed His blessing upon in Scripture were those who were humble. And He removed His leadership mantle from those who lost their humility.

Perhaps this truth can be seen most clearly in the Scriptural comparison between Saul and David in 1 & 2 Samuel. Saul clearly began as a humble leader. When Samuel told Saul that he was God's chosen man to lead His people Saul responded, "But am I not a Benjamite, from the smallest tribe of Israel, and is not my clan the least of all the clans of the tribe of Benjamin? Why do you say such a thing to me?" (1 Sam 9:21)

And after Samuel poured the flask of oil on Saul's head, anointed him king and sent him home we read, "Now Saul's uncle asked him and his servant, 'Where have you been?' 'Looking for the donkeys,' he said. "But when we saw they were not to be found, we went to Samuel." Saul's uncle said, "Tell me what Samuel said to you."

Saul replied, "He assured us that the donkeys had been found." But he did not tell his uncle what Samuel had said about the kingship. (1 Sam 10:14-16)

Finally, when Samuel had brought all the tribes of Israel together Saul was chosen king. But then we read, "But when they looked for him, he was not to be found. So they inquired further of the LORD, "Has the man come here yet?" And the LORD said, "Yes, he has hidden himself among the baggage." (1 Sam 10:21-22)

Certainly Saul began his kingship as a humble man. But then something changed within him. When facing the Philistines, Samuel did not arrive exactly on time to make a promised sacrifice so Saul took matters into his own hands. We read, "So he said, "Bring me the burnt offering and the fellowship offerings. And Saul offered up the burnt offering." (1 Sam 13:9-10)

When Saul attacked the Amalekites God told him to totally destroy them and everything that belonged to them. "But Saul and the army spared Agag and the best of the sheep and cattle, the fat calves and lambs--everything that was good. These they were unwilling to destroy completely." (1 Sam 15:9)

Something had changed within Saul. He lost his humility. We read, "Early in the morning Samuel got up and went to meet Saul, but he was told, 'Saul has gone to Carmel. There he has set up a monument in his own honor and has turned and gone on down to Gilgal.'" (1 Sam 15:12)

Then when Samuel caught him in his act of disobedience, "Then Saul said to Samuel, "I have sinned. I violated the LORD's command and your instructions. I was afraid of the people and so I gave in to them." (1 Sam 15:24) Full of pride, he had selfishly desired the praise of the people more than God's best interests for His children. Saul lost his humility and God removed the mantle of leadership from him. Pathetically, Saul spent the rest of his life trying to hold on to what God had taken away from him only to end up taking his own life in the midst of defeat on Mt. Gilboa. The motives of God's leaders matter deeply to Him.

By contrast, David certainly had many moral failures too. He committed adultery with Bathsheba and then had her husband Uriah murdered. He failed as a parent when his son Amnon raped his daughter Tamar. Absolom, one of David's other sons plotted for two years and then killed Amnon. David failed to deal with Absolom appropriately and in the midst of David's poor administration of the kingdom, Absolom seized David's throne and drove him out of Jerusalem threatening to kill him.

But in the midst of failings like these, somehow David remains the apple of God's eye. Somehow he remains a man after God's own heart.

How? Unlike Saul, David repeatedly humbled himself when confronted with his sin and failure.

For example, as punishment for David's prideful census taking in 2 Samuel 24, God sent a terrible plague among the people. David's response to this reveals his reinstated humility. We read, "When David saw the angel who was striking down the people, he said to the LORD, "I am the one who has sinned and done wrong. These are but sheep. What have they done? Let your hand fall upon me and my family." (2 Sam 24:17) God relented and David remained a man after God's own heart. The motives of God's leaders matter deeply to Him.

But how can we know if we possess appropriate, Godly motives for leading? To answer this question we developed a model that conceptualizes the leadership motives leaders actually possess. What we developed is not simply an intuitive approach. Our model is based on extensive Biblical study, on years of scholarly research that has been published in the Journal of Applied Behavioral Science and on the consulting interactions we've had with thousands of clients.

Simply stated, our model combines the two types of goals we can have in life (selfless or selfish) with the two types of means we can use to reach these goals (sensitive or insensitive). These two dimensions are then combined to form a "Motives for Leading" matrix. The matrix is below:

Motives for Leading Matrix

Means

		Insensitive	Sensitive
Goals	Selfless	Determined Crusader	Humble Servant
	Selfish	Ruthless Maximizer	Sociable Egoist

We believe that God clearly wants His leaders to possess selfless goals (e.g. "Do nothing out of selfish ambition or vain conceit, but in humility consider others better than yourselves. Each of you should look not only to your own interests, but also to the interests of others. (Phil 2:3-4)

We also believe that God wants all of His leaders to use sensitive means (e.g. "Therefore, as God's chosen people, holy and dearly loved, clothe yourselves with compassion, kindness, humility, gentleness and patience. Bear with each other and forgive whatever grievances you may have against one another. Forgive as the Lord forgave you. And over all these virtues put on love, which binds them all together in perfect unity." (Col 3:12-14) Thus we believe that the Humble Servant motive for leading is the one God would have all of His leaders seeking.

As can be seen in the model, there are three other possible motives for leading. The motive least like a humble servant is found in the quadrant labeled Ruthless Maximizer. Leaders in this quadrant are seeking selfish goals and are insensitive toward others as they go about reaching them. Two other motives for leading are Sociable Egoists (leaders having selfish goals, but using sensitive means) and Determined Crusaders (leaders having selfless goals, but using insensitive means). These motives for leading represent a kind of mid-point on a motives for leading continuum. Of course, the Humble Servant quadrant reflects the motives of leaders who have selfless end-goals and who use sensitive means to attain them. It is our belief that this is the quadrant that God desires for His leaders.

In order to better to understand each of these motive profiles, a series of both serious and humorous anecdotes will be offered below. As you read these anecdotes, try to place yourself in one of them. If you would like a more accurate assessment of which quadrant best describes your motives as a leader, you can take an internet survey at www.motivesforleading.com. You will need an access code, however, which can be obtained by an email request to smusser@musserorke.com or to eorke@musserorke.com

Ruthless Maximizers

Leaders who seek to reach selfish goals and use insensitive means.

There is a Christian man we consulted with who grew his organization from five people to over 1,200 in a relatively short number of years. Despite his success, however, his organization has a bad reputation.

Everyone acknowledges that it is not a very nice place to work. One of the reasons for its bad reputation is the behavior of its leader. Like many Ruthless Maximizers, he believes in "self-development." That is, he believes that no one really should need to be trained and developed; that people either have the talent and ability to do something or they don't. He believes that if a person is any good, he or she should be able to do a job without any extra training or development. If he wanted to teach someone how to swim, he'd probably just throw them into the water!

The problem with this approach revealed itself every time he tried to fill a new position. If he needed a new team member, he just put someone into the position. If they couldn't do the job, he fired them. Then he'd put someone else in the position. If that person couldn't do the job, he'd fire him too. He'd repeat this process over and over until he finally found a person who could handle the job. We don't have to tell you how awful most of the people felt who worked there.

One day we received a phone call from a leader in his organization who wanted to know if we would be willing to talk with their Ruthless Maximizer leader about the importance of training his staff. We really didn't want to do it. That's like telling someone to go to a counselor. The person has to want to go for it to be effective. But because we knew the person and could sense the desperation in her voice, we reluctantly agreed.

When we arrived at the organization one Friday morning, the Ruthless Maximizer was waiting for us. He sat behind his desk, leaned back with an air of arrogance and said, "Okay, show me what you got."

We responded by laying out our materials and explaining them to him. He listened for a few minutes and then interrupted. He said, "This all looks very good, but answer me one question. Who made me?" Well, we didn't know how to answer that question so we plowed ahead with our presentation.

He listened patiently for a few minutes and then interrupted us again. He said, "Listen, I told you, this all looks pretty good. But you haven't answered my question. Who made me?"

It was pretty clear what he was trying to communicate. He was arrogantly pointing out that he never had all the specialized training that we were describing and he didn't believe that had hurt him. He had done well for himself. He was a successful leader of his organization. But the people who worked there were miserable and if he couldn't humble himself to help develop his staff, the organization was never going to reach its full potential.

We continued on. As we did he must have interrupted us five or six times, always with the same arrogant question, "Who made me?"

Another associate had come with us to make the presentation whose name was Don. He's a very nice guy, but he's one of those people whose face turns red when they're angry. We noticed that each time the Ruthless Maximizer would ask, "But who made me?" Don would turn a deeper shade of red. The Ruthless Maximizer's arrogance was literally getting under Don's skin.

After several more interruptions Don was glowing. He was about to explode. So when the Ruthless Maximizer asked one last time, "Who made me?"

Don responded with, "Well frankly, no one wants to take the credit and that's why they asked us in here this morning."

We couldn't believe what we had heard. We looked at Don with an expression that said, "You can't talk to leaders like that." But interestingly, the Ruthless Maximizer seemed to like it! Apparently he was impressed that Don had spoken up and was not going to allow him to go on bullying us. From then on we had his attention.

As we discussed things further, he discovered that one of us had a PhD. He said, "You know, when I got out of school I thought about going on to get my "phid" (that's what he called a PhD - a phid)." He said, "But then I thought, 'I could spend all those years studying how to run an organization, or I could go out and build my own.' That's what I did, I built this organization instead."

Once again it was clear what he was implying. He was telling us that real men don't eat quiche and they don't get phids either. Then, to add an arrogant insult to our injury, he said, "And you know what else? I hired two phids last year. They both work for me." I think you'll agree that he was not very selfless or sensitive.

As you can see, Ruthless Maximizers are probably the least humble of the four profiles. This is because they seek their own selfish goals in leading the organization and they often behave very insensitively toward those they interact with to reach these goals. If they are to become one of God's humble servants, it will likely come through God beginning a process to humble them.

If you scored as a Ruthless Maximizer, don't lose hope. God is in the business of transforming lives through the power of His Spirit. The apostle Paul was a Ruthless Maximizer before he met Christ on the road to Damascus. If God was able to transform Paul into a humble servant, he can turn you into one too. There is material at the end of the "Motives for Leading" anecdotes that may help you understand how to change.

Sociable Egoists

Leaders who seek to reach selfish goals but who use sensitive means.

The best example we've ever seen of Sociable Egoists occurred while we were working with a senior leader in a large organization. Because we knew him, we weren't surprised when he called us one day and asked if we'd be willing to do some teambuilding with his leadership team.

We said, "Sure, but what seems to be the problem?"

He said, "I've been working with these people for two years now and they will not work together." Then he added, "If you can't do something with them, I'm going to have to take action. I'm going to have to fire some of them."

"Oh no," we thought. We didn't want to be placed in this type of situation. But since he was a friend, we agreed to work with them.

We gave them the instrument used in our model and then scored it. Six of the seven on his leadership team scored as Sociable Egoists. They were very good at using sensitive means, but they were all seeking selfish goals. That is, they were very nice to each other on the surface. But because they all had selfish goals, they couldn't work well together.

As you might imagine, since they used sensitive means with each other, we had a very good initial meeting. They laughed and joked together as they completed some teambuilding exercises and developed some interpersonal strategies. They made plans to go out to lunch together and we thought the meeting went well.

So when their senior leader asked us about the meeting, we said, "Well it was only the first meeting, but we don't really see a problem. They seem to get along well with each other."

He said, "Don't you believe it. Don't let them do it to you too. They're pulling the wool over your eyes. These people will not work together."

We suggested we give them another instrument where they all offered their opinions and perceptions of each other. What they didn't know was that they were going to see what they had said about each other when the instruments had been scored. We collected the results and sent them to a company in Minneapolis for tabulation and interpretation. A few days later we got a call from the company asking us if we had received the results in the mail. We told them that they had arrived that morning but that we didn't get a chance to look at them.

They said, "Well, we strongly recommend that you do not give the results back to those people."

We were stunned and asked, "Why not?"

They said, "Because in our experience with over 25,000 leaders in our database, we never had a group of people assassinate each other the way they did!"

We thought, "Oh boy, just what we needed."

We called their boss, the senior leader, and said, "We have good news and bad news. Which do you want to hear first?"

He said, Give me the good news." We said, "The good news is that the surveys from your leadership team have come in."

He said, "Great! How do they look?"

"That's the bad news," we said. We told him that the company doing the scoring recommended that we not give the results back to them.

He said, "Not give them back? Why not? We paid over $3,500 to complete and score those surveys."

We had to tell him the truth. We said, "Well, the company who scored them said that in their experience with over 25,000 leaders, they never had a group assassinate each other the way your people did."

There was silence on the other end of the phone for a long time. Then he said to us, "You give the results back to them. This is exactly what I've been telling them they are doing and I want them to see it for themselves."

"Okay," we said. "It's your call."

We went into the meeting room with his leadership team the next day.

We passed out the results and then slowly backed up against the wall. We didn't want to be in harm's way if a fight broke out.

They reacted strongly to the results at first. One of them said, "You creep, Phil. Tell me you said this. You scum!" And then he said, "Hey, what are you doing at three this afternoon? Want to go shoot a couple holes of golf together?"

Eventually, everyone began responding the same way. There was some initial anger at first, but then their sensitive means took over. Before long the whole group was laughing and joking with each other again. They truly were Sociable Egoists. They were all out for themselves (selfish end goals), but they tried to be so nice in the way they went about it (sensitive means). Unfortunately, it ended up that their boss, the senior leader, felt it necessary to fire four of them. Why? Because they were Sociable Egoists.

This may be an interesting story, but our experience with many Christians reflects a similar outcome. We have found that many Christians seem to possess the Sociable Egoist profile. It seems that their faith doesn't always impact their goals to be any different from those of unbelievers. They are both caught up with the narcissism of our culture and they both seek more selfish goals in life like power, wealth and status.

Where their faith does seem to make a difference is in the means many choose to reach their selfish goals. They try to be kind, caring and compassionate in their dealing with others. But this is not enough. This is not the true humility God seeks in His servants. It is admirable to use sensitive means, but God also wants us to be seeking selfless goals.

Determined Crusaders

Leaders who seek to reach selfless goals but who use insensitive means.

People with this profile are a sort of a mirror opposite of Sociable Egoists. They seek selfless goals, but they nevertheless fall short of becoming Humble Servants because they tend to use insensitive means to reach them. That is, they become focused more on effectiveness and the bottom line in reaching their selfless goals than they do on being sensitive to the needs of those around them.

We knew a senior leader once who definitely had selfless goals.

Seeking the Pillar of Fire

When she became the senior leader she put her office in the middle of the second floor of the organization's headquarters. This was very different from her predecessors who were always located in the palatial surroundings of the eleventh floor.

As you might imagine, the people working in the organization found their Determined Crusader senior leader to be a refreshing alternative to the Ruthless Maximizers they had worked for in the past. The people were amazed that their leader would be willing to have an office in the center of the second floor without any windows. Everyone there knew that in the past, anyone who was important had an office with a window and that those who were very important had corner offices where there were two windows. But not this Determined Crusader. She was selfless. She was out for the good of the people.

She even got rid of all the private parking spaces. She declared at one meeting, "No more special treatment for senior level leaders. From now on it's first come, first serve when it comes to parking." And she was often the one worst affected. Because of her irregular hours, she often had to park in the far corner of the parking lot and tromp through the rain and snow to get inside the building.

Needless to say, the people really wanted to love this woman. She seemed refreshingly humble. But there was a problem. It wasn't her goals that were problematic. It was the means she used to attain them. As a Determined Crusader, she chose to use insensitive means to reach her selfless goals. Perhaps an example might help to illustrate.

She met us in front of her office door one Monday morning and said, "Oh, we tried to reach you before you left, but I guess we couldn't get through. We're not going to be able to meet today, I had to schedule another meeting. But listen, while you're here, why don't you sit in on the meeting. Maybe it'll give you some ideas."

Since we were already there we said, "Sure, we'd love to."

The meeting turned out to be pretty interesting. There were six senior level leaders there with her and they were trying to decide whether or not to build a new facility at a particular geographic location. Each one of the senior level leaders gave a report from his or her functional perspective concerning the feasibility of building the facility.

We noticed that the Determined Crusader didn't let anyone finish reporting. When they were about half-way finished she'd cut them off

50

and say, "I think we get the picture. Anything else really important you wanted to say? If not, let's move on to the next report." It was as if she had her mind already made up and just wanted to get the meeting over with.

But then she shocked us. After the last report she said, "Okay, I think we have enough information. It's time to make the decision. Let's take a vote." When she said, "Let's take a vote," we were shocked. Taking a vote is a sensitive means to reaching a goal. It didn't fit her profile.

She said, "Everyone who is in favor of building the new facility, put your hand up." She was the only one who put her hand up. She looked puzzled perhaps wondering if there were any abstentions. So she said, "Okay, everybody who is opposed to building the facility, put your hand up." All six senior level leaders raised their hands.

She got a puzzled look on her face for just a moment and then said, "No, we're gonna build it anyway." You can imagine the look on the faces of the other leaders.

As we were walking down the hall together toward her office, she apparently got a little embarrassed and said, "Well, I guess you're wondering what just went on in there."

We said, "As a matter of fact, yes we are. There were six votes against building. You were the only one in favor and yet you're going to go ahead and build the new facility anyway."

She then got a clever little smile on her face and said, "Well, let me tell you guys how it is around here." She said, "Some days we count the votes and other days we weigh them. Today we weighed the votes." And then she laughed a little laugh that only a Determined Crusader could think was funny.

But the six senior level leaders didn't think it was very funny. One woman said, "She does this all the time. She already knows what she wants to do before she ever comes into a meeting. We go through these silly charades and it's humiliating. Why doesn't she just tell what she's going to do and let us all get on with it? That would be a lot easier and lot less frustrating."

Another senior level leader said, "It's like she likes to rub our noses in it."

But these responses misstate her intentions. As a Determined Crusader, she had selfless goals. She wanted only what was best for the organization, for the workers, and for the public. She wasn't concerned at all with selfish goals like power and status. What repeatedly got her into so much trouble with her leadership team was her use of insensitive means to reach these goals.

If you looked at where she put her office and where she parked her car, you might be tempted to think she was a Humble Servant. But she wasn't. She had selfless goals. But she could be very insensitive with her leadership team as she sought to do what she believed was best for the organization.

Once we were doing some work for a large missions organization. The man who was in charge had developed a wonderful program for reaching the people in his mission field with the gospel of Christ. His heart beat with the selfless goal of evangelizing and bringing people into the kingdom. But he too was a Determined Crusader. Like the previous senior leader, he wasn't concerned with the trappings of leadership and authority. He also had a modest little office and very little material possessions.

But the missionaries who served under him were beginning to leave the field in alarming numbers. Many of them were leaving because of the way he tended to treat them. They felt marginalized, unappreciated and unworthy under his leadership. He was unintentionally causing them to question their calling.

You see, in his passion for reaching the lost with the gospel, this Determined Crusader became insensitive to the missionaries' need to be loved, encouraged and supported. All he could see was the goal of evangelism.

When we spoke with him, we told him that he was not a Humble Servant. He looked at us with shock on his face. He didn't understand. He had given up everything to serve Christ on the mission field. He had not thought about his needs or welfare, but only about the spiritual needs of the lost all around him. He couldn't believe he was not a Humble Servant.

We assured him that his selfless goals were pleasing to God. But we also told him that the insensitive means he used to reach these goals were not pleasing at all to God. We explained to him that to truly be a Humble Servant, a person needed not only to have selfless goals, but to also use sensitive means to reach them.

Humble Servants

Leaders who seek to reach selfless goals and who use sensitive means.

One Humble Servant leader of a very large organization we know of was having a meeting with his senior leadership team. During the lively, interactive meeting this Humble Servant mostly sat back and let the team run the meeting.

Around mid-morning, he interrupted them and asked if anyone would like to place an order for coffee and a donut. As the people on his leadership team gave their orders, he dutifully recorded them on a little pad of paper. When everyone had ordered, he quietly slipped out of the room and the meeting continued.

About a half hour later he entered the room with his top coat still on carrying a large paper bag. He asked the team if this was a good time to take a break and then proceeded to serve the coffee and donuts they had ordered.

At lunch, one of the leaders at the meeting approached him and asked with incredulity in her voice, "You actually went out and got the coffee and donuts yourself didn't you?" He said, "Yes, is that surprising to you?" She said, "Well you're the senior leader of the team. How come you didn't just give the order to a secretary and let her get the coffee and donuts?" He looked at her with a rather surprised look on his face and said, "Well you saw how well the meeting was going. I simply thought I'd try to make myself useful." You see, he had a Humble Servant motive for leading. He sought to fulfill selfless goals and tried to be sensitive to the needs of the people he led.

But sometimes having a Humble Servant motive for leading isn't all that simple. There was a once a senior leader we consulted with who was faced with a very difficult situation. After leading her organization for only three years she was faced with fulfilling the selfless goal of letting 125 of her staff go for the good of the overall organization. This move was made necessary by financial circumstances beyond her control. But to make the situation worse, many of the people being let go had worked for the organization for over 20 years.

Because she had a Humble Servant motive for leading, she was determined to do all she could to help those who were being let go. As a result she decided to let them know a full year before they were going to be released. Many had concerns that such a move might result in low productivity or even sabotage during the coming year. Nevertheless, she was committed to doing what she felt was the right and best thing for these people.

She also immediately set up a process to help those who were being let go to obtain other positions outside her organization. But she didn't stop there. She was so concerned with their emotional and psychological well-being, that at considerable expense, she arranged for a counselor to meet with groups of people to help them work through their feelings and concerns.

While we were doing some work in her organization during this time we heard from the counselor that he was hearing some very interesting and surprising comments from the people meeting with him. He told us that we probably wouldn't believe him if he told us what they were saying so he invited us to sit in on one of the sessions.

As the meeting began, he asked the soon to be laid off workers what they were feeling. Their responses ranged from fear and anxiety to feeling abandoned and alone. Many of them said that they felt like a husband or wife who had come home to find out that their spouse had left them. They didn't know what they were going to do in the future or where they were going to go.

But then, almost to a person, they said something that shocked us to the core. They said that although they were fearful and worried about the future, "If this Humble Servant senior leader made such a decision, then we're sure it had to be." What was so amazing about this response was the deep level of trust it reflected. This woman had just turned their lives upside down. She had pulled the rug out from under them and yet they were able to say that if she made the decision to do this, then they felt sure it was the right decision regardless of its consequences for them. And it was not just one or two of the workers who said this. It was virtually all of them.

We know of no higher compliment that a leader can be paid than for people to express such deep personal trust in the face of leadership decisions that are devastating to workers' lives. These workers trusted their senior leader's decisions because of her character – because of the Humble Servant motive for leading she had demonstrated over the past three years. For her, leadership was not just about seeking selfless goals that were good for the overall organization. It was also about the sensitive way people need to be treated while reaching such goals.

A Biblical Model of Personal Change

The first thing one needs to understand about the process of becoming humble is that it is the work of God in our lives. We can't make ourselves humble – it is the work of God. But He does give us freedom in this process – freedom to yield or freedom to resist His efforts.

The second thing one needs to understand is that God often seems to use a specific process to bring us to humility. And this process seems to have three basic phases. The first phase involves God letting us experience "significant loss." This loss can take many forms. It can be a serious health issue, a financial crisis, the loss of a job or a broken relationship. It is a journey into the desert of suffering.

It's interesting to note that virtually every one of the leaders in Scripture that God called to lead, He allowed to experience the desert. Moses spent 40 years in the wilderness of Midian. David lived for years like a wild animal hiding in caves and fleeing from his enemies. Elijah watched in horror as the Brook Kerith dried up. Jeremiah experienced rejection and hatred. And Paul experienced blindness, persecution and a thorn in the flesh.

What is the purpose of God allowing His leaders to experience significant loss? There are undoubtedly many purposes God might have for sending us into the desert of suffering. But He often seems to use these times of loss to cause His leaders to totally set aside their self-dependence and to yield their wills to His. That is, He often allows His leaders to experience significant loss to give them the opportunity of choosing brokenness before Him.

This second phase of the humility process is perhaps the most critical. For it is in the choosing of brokenness, through the work of the Holy Spirit, that we come to set aside our wills, our needs and our wants to be replaced with God's desire for our lives.

This brokenness before God can be likened to what occurs when a horse is broken before its rider. When the horse finally surrenders its will to that of the rider, brokenness has its full effect. From then on if the horse wants to run, but the rider wants it to stop, the horse will stop. If the horse wants to stop, but the rider wants it to run, it will run. If it wants to go to the left, but the rider leads to the right, it will follow and obey.

And this brokenness does not lessen the horse's joy. Indeed, the horse's joy and fulfillment are heightened. For it is only when the horse is joined to the rider in total submission, that the horse can accomplish great feats and great achievements.

Then, through God's amazing transforming power, He uses the submission of our will to His to enable us to set aside our needs for the sake of others. That is, God molds our brokenness to Him into humility toward others. This is the last and final phase of God's work to make us Humble Servants.

There are some wonderful examples of Humble Servants in Scripture. As mentioned, they include people like Moses and David and Paul. But God sent each of these saints into the desert of trial and tribulation at some point in their lives. And as they fell on their faces in the desert offering God nothing more than crushed wills, He created the humility in them that was so very necessary to serve Him.

It doesn't matter if you are currently a Ruthless Maximizer, a Sociable Egoist or a Determined Crusader. God is able to turn anyone into a Humble Servant the way he did these men and so many others in Scripture. But we must follow their example. We too must fall on our faces before God and offer Him nothing more and nothing less than crushed wills. Perhaps you find yourself in the desert of trial and tribulation right now. If you do, then try to learn the lesson of humility that God wants you to learn – the lesson He wants all of His leaders to learn.

An Admonition

Finally, we need to seriously caution you before reading further. Our research suggests that most Christians do not fall into the Humble Servant quadrant when they take our survey. Nevertheless the critical thing is whether you are moving toward or away from the Humble Servant profile. If you sense that your motives for leading are moving away from those of a Humble Servant, we would strongly urge you NOT to seek to implement the process that will be defined in the next set of chapters. It is far more important that you first devote yourself to prayer, reflection and brokenness before God. Allow Him to move you toward the Humble Servant He desires you to be. If you proceed to implement the process defined in the next set of chapters with improper motives, you are likely to do more harm than good to your church.

However, even if you don't believe the Humble Servant profile best describes you at this time, if you are allowing God to "move you toward" becoming a Humble Servant through brokenness and submission, we believe you should feel free move forward with implementing what is described in the next set of chapters in your church. That is, we believe it is not so much where you are on the profile matrix that matters as much as what direction you are allowing God to move you. For example, we believe that David certainly was not always a Humble Servant. But his life was characterized by a willingness to submit himself in brokenness to God and to allow God repeatedly to move him toward becoming a Humble Servant.

This would be a good time to go before God in prayer and ask Him to reveal to you whether you are moving toward or away from becoming a Humble Servant. This may be the single most important thing you may do as a result of reading this book.

Chapter 8
Engaging the Leadership Community

As was discussed earlier, we believe that all churches share the same Biblical mission of glorifying God by helping people become more like Jesus and by fulfilling the Great Commission. God also gives each local church a vision that reflects the distinctive contribution He wants that church to make to the mosaic of churches that comprise the church universal. Because a local church's God-given vision is at least distinctive, if not unique, there are a great variety of local church visions within the church universal. However, all of these diverse visions serve to fulfill a common purpose, a common mission.

As was alluded to in chapters 1, 2 and 6, we believe that the process of uncovering God's vision and direction for one of His local churches should be a broad process that minimally includes the pastor, the senior leadership and at least some of the congregation. The remaining chapters will lay out a simple, but powerful approach that a local church can follow to utilize all of these people in uncovering God's vision/ direction.

The first step is to define the composition of what we call the Leadership Community (hereafter LC) in a local church. We recommend that it be comprised of all those in the church who meet at least one of the following qualifications:

a. every elder, deacon, paid staff member, church council member or other "senior" level leader within the church.

b. every volunteer who has the overall responsibility for leading a ministry at your church – no matter how large or small (e.g. director of children's ministry, director women's ministry, director of men's ministry, food pantry, etc.).

c. every one who leads others in ministry under the oversight of your ministry pastoral staff and directors (e.g. Vacation Bible

School leaders, Children's Sunday School leaders, etc.).

d. every one who fulfills some type of teaching ministry role in the church (e.g., Adult Bible Fellowship (ABF) leaders, small group leaders, Sunday School teachers, etc.).

Once the LC has been defined, the next step is to arrange "focus group" meetings with these individuals. We recommend the focus group meetings be comprised of roughly 12 people each. We have found that it is not necessary to form the focus groups around clusters of people who share the same ministry interest and service. Focus groups made up of people from a variety of ministry interests and service perform just as well as those made up of people with the same ministry interests and service.

People from the LC should be assigned a specific date and time for the focus group meeting they are to attend. However, if someone can't make that assigned date and time they can be encouraged to come to one of the other meetings as an alternative. We strongly recommend that these meetings not exceed 75 minutes. So, on a week night, two focus group meetings could be scheduled at 6:30 PM and at 8:00 PM.

The person leading the focus group meetings should be someone who is respected within the church and who obviously has a good rapport when interacting with others. Clearly experience in leading meetings is also a great plus. Our personal practice has been to have one of our staff lead each focus group, but depending on your church's denomination and preferences, you could choose someone from within the church itself.

At the meeting itself, after a brief introduction and warm-up, the person leading the focus group should ask participants to respond to each of the questions below one at a time:

a. What do you believe are two or three of the greatest gifts God has given this church?

b. What do you believe are two or three of the greatest opportunities God may presenting this church at this time?

c. What is your God-given dream for this church?

We have found it most effective to present the group with the first question without letting them see the second and third question and to have them finish working on the first question before introducing the second question, and so on. We ask people to first briefly write down their answers and then to break into subgroups of three or four and share their responses with the others in their subgroup. We then ask each subgroup to choose what the group believes to be the two or three best responses from their subgroup and share them with the focus group as a whole.

The pastor, who is asked to attend all of the focus group meetings, is the one who then faithfully and dutifully records all the responses the subgroups share. It is important to note that the pastor's role during these focus group meetings should be strictly limited to listening and recording the feedback from the subgroups. The pastor can ask a clarifying question to make sure he is accurately recording the subgroup's response but he should not engage in discussion or dialogue. The pastor is there only to listen and record. As you will see later, this is critical to the process.

The second question is presented to the subgroup the same way the first one was and the subgroup should follow the same process for responding to question two as they did in responding to question one. The process for the third question, however, is quite different.

When presenting the focus group with question number three we have found it most effective to not use subgroup discussion. We have found the best way to get responses to question number three is to first, simply present them with the question; second, ask them to individually pray and reflect on how God would have them answer it; and third, ask them to share their responses individually before the whole focus group. However, no one should be required to share. It is best to simply open up the time for anyone to share what God has laid on their hearts in answer to the question. We have found, nevertheless, that almost everyone does indeed share his or her response to question number three.

After they have had a chance to share we recommend the meeting end by thanking them for their time and input and by asking one of them to close in prayer. The process is then repeated with another focus group. We usually recommend about a fifteen minute break between the ending of one group and the beginning of another to assure a smooth transition.

By the end of all of the focus group meetings, the pastor should have a rather extensive packet of feedback responses. These responses will be a critical resource in the next step of the process as will be discussed

Chapter 9
The Pastor's "Ascent up the Mountain"

Thus far we have made the case that one leader receives the vision from the Lord and brings it to the rest of the leadership team and it is then shared with the congregation. The question is: among the leaders in the church, which one receives the vision? While the Bible doesn't describe the exact leadership structure for the local church it does, however, provide information necessary for developing principles about church governance.

1 Timothy 5:17 states that "The elders who direct the affairs of the church are worthy of double honor, especially those whose work is preaching and teaching." It is clear from this verse that there is a single group of elders and all of them have a role in leading the church. However, some are freed up to preach and teach – to serve as the senior teaching pastor.

We also see that there was a position among the New Testament elders that we would call the "chairman" today. That position was held by James. When Peter miraculously escaped from prison as recorded in Acts 12 he went to the house of Mary the mother of John where people were praying for him. And he said to them, "Tell James and the brothers about this." (Acts 12:17b) Later in the life of the early church Paul and his missionary team returned to Jerusalem after his third journey. Acts 21: 17-19 records, "When we arrived in Jerusalem, the brothers received us warmly. The next day Paul and the rest of us went to see James, and all the elders were present. Paul greeted them and reported in detail what God had done among the Gentiles through his ministry."

The Bible describes a leadership structure where all the elders as a group are to direct the affairs of the church. Within this group there are lay elders, "preaching/teaching elders" (which we argue are pastors today) and a chairman or moderator. In the early church neither James, the chairman, nor the elder board as a whole were the ones God chose to reveal His vision for the church. Instead, God revealed it to the preaching elder. God's revealing of his vision was discussed in Chapters 3 and 5. Peter, who was the preaching elder, received the sheet vision introducing Gentiles into the church and the rest of the elders embraced the vision (Acts 10 and 11). In Acts 15 Paul and Barnabas, also preaching elders, presented their position regarding the Gentiles to the Council at Jerusalem. The elders listened and accepted Paul and Barnabas' position as their own. The point is that once again it was the "preaching elders" who God graced with His vision.

Therefore, as we work with the churches in our district, we have recommended that the senior pastor set apart a time to withdraw from daily ministry to seek God's face and to uncover God's direction, God's vision for the church. Quite frankly, many pastors find this to be rather intimidating. They feel the pressure of high expectations as the elders, the church's leadership community and the entire congregation wait for them to come down "from the mountain" and share God's direction for their church.

They often ask, "What if I don't discern God's leading; what if I come back without having heard clearly from God?" Their anxiety doesn't come from a belief that God will not speak to them but rather from a real concern that they may not hear Him clearly. Nevertheless, it is with a deep sense of gratitude to our God that we can report that all the pastors who have taken part in the process we are describing have come back to their boards with a compelling vision for the future of their church.

The most important aspect in this process of discerning the vision is to first involve all the church leadership and the entire congregation in concerted prayer. The vision of a local church is never developed by working through a series of techniques. Instead, discerning God's vision for the church is a spiritual exercise which requires a congregation to be on its knees as the pastor goes away to spend time with God. In the very beginning of the church the believers devoted themselves to prayer. Acts 4 :24a describes believers who "raised their voices together in prayer to God." Today when the pastor goes on retreat to discern God's vision for the church we believe it is absolutely essential that the entire church also "raise their voices together in prayer to God."

This type of corporate prayer can take many forms. Certainly each member can and should commit individually to pray for the pastor. There also can be prayer meetings at church or in homes. A 24-hour prayer vigil can be designed where members pray at a certain hour the entire time the pastor is away. E-mail prayer reminders can be sent out. Each church will handle this differently, but each church must commit to wholehearted prayer during the process.

With the congregation praying for him, the pastor goes away to a secluded spot for 1 ½ to 2 days. Many times someone in the church will have a cabin or other location that is suitable. The pastor brings only his Bible, the notes he has taken at the Leadership Community focus groups and perhaps a devotional book. This is to be a deeply spiritual time of communing with God. The pastor's goal simply is to reflect and pray about the things that God is showing him in Scripture as well as that which God has been speaking into the hearts of the Leadership Community. It is not a time to read books or articles on leadership, vision or what other churches are doing. Rather, it is a time to spend in wonderful communion with God seeking His direction for the church.

What the pastors who have taken part in these vision retreats have found to be so releasing is that the process really was not dependent on them – not on their skills or their personality or their creativity. Rather it was God speaking to them with His vision for their church as they were being held up in prayer by the church family.

We believe that while all leadership in a local church is responsible to communicate and implement the vision, it is important to recognize that ultimately, the "vision of a local church must reside in the pulpit." The preaching pastor who has received the vision from God is the one who has the best opportunity and responsibility, week in and week out, to communicate the vision from the pulpit and to call the congregation to action. This doesn't mean that each Sunday a "vision sermon" is preached. It simply means that each Sunday some aspect of the worship service draws people toward the direction that God has given their church.

Examples of vision statements:

There is no pattern or form that the vision has to take other than being short enough that it can be easily remembered and focused enough to provide clear direction for action. The vision is not a "slogan," it is a simple statement of the direction in which God is leading. The following examples might help illustrate this point.

(1) An established church with strong teaching and healthy body life saw God call them to open their heart and ministry to the community: *"To be a church whose people develop genuine, redemptive relationships with seekers and whose programs consistently provide a variety of opportunities for seekers to take their next step toward Jesus."*

(2) A small church with a solid ministry saw God lead them to focus on personal spiritual growth leading to outreach: *"Becoming Inviting People to be Inviting People."*

(3) God led a very large church in our district to fulfill a vision for outreach by: *"Becoming a church that flows deep and wide into our community with God's truth."*

(4) God gave still another church the following vision: *"To become a I Thessalonians 2:8 Church" (to love people so much that we are delighted to share with them not only the gospel of God but our lives as well.)*

(5) To yet another church God revealed His vision to them as: *"To truly become a church that is a "light on a hill; a light to the world."*

We have discovered that while perhaps few of these visions may seem particularly exciting or compelling to people outside of these churches, these visions nevertheless often became deeply moving expressions of God's direction to people inside them. When these visions were shared, there sometimes was sobbing among the congregations. We believe that what made these local church visions so compelling to their congregations was not how "clever" or how "savvy" the visions sounded. Instead what made them so powerful was first, these local church visions were uncovered through an inclusive and deeply spiritual process that genuinely sought God's leading through prayer. And second, there was a general consensus that these visions had come directly from God. Because of the process employed, no one seriously questioned whether the vision had come from the minds of the leaders rather than from God.

Once God's direction for a local church has been uncovered, it should then become the foundation for many critical decisions. These include, but are not limited to staffing strategies, succession planning and ministry development. But we believe the most important outcome of uncovering God's vision for a local church is the role it plays in enabling the church to develop a strategic plan. This is the subject of Chapter 10.

Chapter 10
Preparing to Cross into the Promised Land

I worked with a church one time that was, at its core, a very solid church. The pastor was an exceptional preacher, the leaders were Godly and committed, the congregation was blessed with many gifts and talents and the physical facilities were above average. Just as importantly, they successfully had "sought the pillar of fire" using the process discussed in the previous chapters and believed they had clearly received God's direction for their church. But the church never seemed to go to the next level. Attendance slowly increased but everyone felt that something was clearly missing. Despite uncovering God's vision for their church not much changed. As time went on many became discouraged and began to question whether they had really heard from God.

I received a call from the pastor one day asking whether I would be available to lead them in another round of seeking to uncover God's vision for them. I was surprised by the request. I asked, "Didn't you already go through the process of uncovering God's vision for your church?" The pastor responded, "Yes, but we really haven't seen much change in the church as a result. That's why we'd like to try one more time."

I really didn't like what I was hearing. I asked, "Before we go through the process again, tell me what you've done so far to implement the vision into your church." He said, "Well, we rolled out the vision to the congregation on a Sunday evening like you suggested. We had a meal together first and then prayed together that God would help to fulfill the wonderful vision He had given to us. Then we held a meeting with all of the ministry leaders in the church to make sure they understood the vision and to answer any questions or concerns they might have. Next, we asked each of them to make a commitment to seek to implement the vision in each of their ministries. Everyone, the elders, the ministry leaders and the rest of the congregation were excited to see what God was going to do. But frankly, not much seemed to happen beyond the addition of a few banners in the sanctuary and some reprinting of our literature to reflect the "vision."

I suggested that it might be wise for him and me to meet together for breakfast sometime soon to talk more about this. He agreed and we met a few days later. At that breakfast, I pointed out one glaring omission that his church had made. After they had uncovered God's vision for them, they never generated and implemented a strategic plan to help the church move toward fulfilling it.

When I said this I noticed the pastor grew quiet and kept looking down at his coffee. "What's the matter?" I asked. "I hope I haven't offended you. Failing to generate and implement a strategic plan to fulfill the vision happens often among churches."

"That's not it." he said. "You haven't offended me."

"Well, then what seems to be troubling you?" I asked.

He said, "I really don't believe in strategic planning within the church. I feel it's a business tactic that really doesn't belong in God's churches. I believe very strongly in the sovereignty of God regarding the future and how His Spirit moves to accomplish His plans. Strategic planning seems to ignore this. It seems to imply that we humans can influence the future as much as, or maybe even more than God. That's why strategic planning in the church troubles me so much."

I thanked him for his frankness and told him that his response had helped me understand a great deal. But then I asked him, "Despite what you've just shared with me, would you at least be open to hearing a different point of view on the subject of strategic planning within the church?" He graciously agreed without hesitation. "I really don't want to be dogmatic about this. Sure, talk to me." he said.

I said, "Let's begin with a rather important basic assumption. That assumption is that God not only isn't opposed to planning, He seems to use it and promote it." I pointed out to him that God Himself is a planner. We see this throughout the Scriptures. I drew him to Genesis, chapter one where we are shown that God had a clear plan when He created the universe and everything in it.

Even after man had fallen into sin in Genesis chapter three, God immediately responds with a plan.

So the LORD God said to the serpent, "Because you have done this, "Cursed are you above all the livestock and all the wild animals! You will crawl on your belly and you will eat dust all the days of your life. And I will put enmity between you and the woman, and between your offspring and hers; he will crush your head, and you will strike his heel. (Gen 3:14-15)

As soon as man sinned, God shared His plan for the forgiveness of our sins through the sacrifice of His Son.

I pointed out that God also had a strategy for creating a people for Himself through the offspring of Abraham. He had a strategy for bringing Israel out of Egypt and into the Promised Land. He had a strategy for bringing salvation to the Gentiles as He created the Church.

The pastor interrupted me, "But you're making my point! It is God who does the strategic planning, not us!" I then reminded him that I was simply making the point that strategic planning in itself is not something that is reprehensible to God.

I also pointed out to him that the Scriptural examples of strategic planning are not limited to those accomplished by God. Abraham developed strategies, Moses developed strategies, Joshua developed strategies, Gideon developed strategies, David developed strategies, Nathan developed a strategy, Elijah developed strategies, Esther developed a strategy, Nehemiah developed strategies, Peter developed strategies, Paul developed strategies and so did many, many others in the Bible.

The pastor said, "Okay, okay…I think I see the point you're trying to make. Maybe my problem is that I really haven't understood what strategic planning looks like. How do you define it? What does it entail?"

I began by sharing that our simple definition of a strategic plan is, "*a logical and detailed plan that helps direct a church to intentionally and thoughtfully do things that seem beneficial to fulfilling God's vision for it.*" As can be seen in this definition, a strategic plan is not an attempt to direct the church into a direction that either the leaders or the congregation have decided upon. To the contrary, it is a plan to move the church in a direction or onto a path toward the kind of church God has revealed He wants it to be.

"Well, I can't argue with that definition of a strategic plan." the pastor said. "But who actually generates this plan and what does the process for generating it look like?"

We believe that one of the most frequent mistakes that churches make when they engage in strategic planning is choosing the wrong people to do it. Many of the churches we've worked with believe that strategic planning is the responsibility of the Elder Board. Since the strategic plan is critical in accomplishing the direction of the church, they believe that it is only the elders who should do such planning. Unfortunately, there is a critical flaw in this logic.

When we've met with elder boards who believe it is their responsibility to generate the church's strategic plan, we usually ask them these simple questions, "When you need surgery, who do you seek to perform it? When the transmission in your car starts dropping parts all over the highway, who do you ask to fix it? When the central air conditioner in your house begins blowing warm air, who do you call to repair it?"

The usual responses to these questions are doctors (surgeons), auto mechanics and HVAC technicians. We respond by telling them that they are correct. They turn over their need to professionals – to experts – to people who have been trained to understand what is needed. The same is true in generating a strategic plan. The people who should have the responsibility for generating and implementing a strategic plan in the church are those who have the most expertise in understanding the nuances and intricacies of various ministries; those who are reading, going to conferences and developing themselves in various ministries.

Therefore, it is our belief that the group of people best able to generate an effective strategic plan within the church to fulfill God's vision for it is what we call the Leadership Core. The Leadership Core is comprised of all of the major ministry leaders within the church. For example, we believe the Leadership Core should include the Senior Pastor, the Worship Leader, the leader of Youth Ministry, the leader of Children's Ministry, the leader of Young Adult Ministry, the leader of Missions, the leader of Discipleship Ministry, the leader of Women's Ministry, the leader of Men's Ministry, the leader of Prayer Ministry, etc. Obviously, the makeup of each local church's Leadership Core will look different depending on what major ministries exist in that church.

The reason that we believe the Leadership Core of the church should generate the strategic plan is two-fold. First, as discussed earlier, these are the people who usually have the greatest ministry experience, training and insight in their areas. Second, these are the very people who will be called upon to implement the strategic plan within the church. Their ownership of the strategic plan through having generated it is critical to the effectiveness of implementation.

The pastor then said, "You mean there is no role at all for the Elder Board in the church's strategic planning process?" I assured him that there was indeed a role for them – a critically important role. The elders are the ones who will be called upon to approve the strategic plan the Leadership Core develops. They are also the ones to whom the Leadership Core will be responsible for implementation of the plan. Further, it is the role of the elders to periodically assess the effectiveness of the plan in moving the church toward fulfilling its God-given vision and to require the Leadership Core to make whatever adjustments might be necessary.

The pastor asked, "But how does the Leadership Core actually generate the church's strategic plan? I love my ministry leaders, but sometimes trying to get them to all pull together in the same direction is about as easy as trying to herd cats!" I assured him that this was an excellent question and that I'd be sure to cover it with him the next time we met.

The process whereby the Leadership Core of a church generates its strategic plan is critically important. That is why we've chosen to make the discussion and delineation of this process the subject matter of Chapter 11.

Chapter 11
Taking Possession of the Promised Land

Developing the strategic plan involves both full dependence on God for wisdom and direction as well as strong commitment and hard work by the Leadership Core. The Leadership Core will meet regularly, usually twice a month, for anywhere from six to twelve months to develop the plan. Members of the Leadership Core must commit to attend each meeting, work on the plan between meetings, and pray fervently for the process. Also, others in leadership and the entire congregation will also be asked to commit to pray regularly for them and the planning process. The final product will be God's plan for the church to reach its vision as developed through the hard work of the Leadership Core.

A wonderful example of dependence on God through prayer and hard work to fulfill a vision is recorded in Nehemiah. As Nehemiah and the people of Jerusalem worked to rebuild the walls, opposition plotted against them. Their response was "…we prayed to our God and posted a guard day and night to meet this threat." (Nehemiah 4:9) They trusted in God and did the work that they needed to do to provide defense, and the wall was completed in fifty-two days. Vision fulfilled!

The leader of the strategic planning process is best described as a facilitator. He/she guides the Leadership Core through the planning process, asks questions, clarifies, and moves it along so that it does not become bogged down. The facilitator, however, does not provide input into the actual goals and objectives being developed. He/she must seek to remain as impartial and objective as possible in processing the contributions and ideas so that the final plan is solely the product of the Leadership Core. Quite frankly, this role can be difficult especially if the facilitator is a church member with ideas he/she feels should be incorporated into the plan. It requires a great amount of restraint to hold back. While the process certainly can be led successfully by someone within the church, it is our experience that most churches prefer to have someone outside the church, such as a member of the district leadership team, facilitate the process.

Setting the Stage

At the first meeting it is crucial that each member of the Leadership Core develops an understanding of the planning process they will be part of over the coming months. The facilitator should review the following, answer questions and encourage the members about the importance of their task.

1. Carefully answer the question asked in Chapter 10 – "Is strategic planning just another business technique that doesn't really belong in the church?" Some members of the Leadership Core may be struggling with this.

2. Define a strategic plan as "a logical and detailed plan that helps direct a church to intentionally and thoughtfully do things that seem beneficial to fulfilling God's vision for it."

3. Help them understand that a strategic plan is something that provides many benefits to the church as it seeks to fulfill the ministry God has called it to accomplish.

- *A strategic plan provides structure.* While churches should be willing to empower people to do ministry in ways that utilize their God-given talents and gifts, there still needs to be a "game plan" so that their efforts are aligned with the church's vision. A strategic plan provides this alignment.

- *A strategic plan helps leaders to articulate their ideas.* As the Leadership Cores interacts in the strategic planning process, they are forced to clearly articulate their ideas in the form of a written strategic plan. This written, clearly articulated plan is essential for the congregation to understand and embrace the church's future direction. Although strategic planning is hard and sometimes tedious work, the results it produces are well worth the effort.

- *A strategic plan organizes the efforts of those serving in ministry.* A strategic plan identifies "what" people are going to do and "who" will be doing it.

- *A strategic plan enables effective team building to occur.* As the Leadership Core interacts in the development of the strategic plan, their cohesiveness often increases as they work together for the good of the church as a whole.

• *A strategic plan eliminates confusion and saves time.* When there is a well defined plan in place the people implementing the plan find clarity on what has to be done and when. Confusion and the resulting frustration it produces are reduced significantly.

• *A strategic plan can help ministry recruitment.* When people in the congregation know where the church is headed and how it going to get there they are usually more willing to get involved. A good strategic plan generates excitement within the church and increases many people's willingness to serve.

• *A strategic plan improves assimilation.* When visitors consider joining a church a good strategic plan enables them to more clearly assess if this is the church God is leading them to serve in.

4. Share the key principles of strategic planning with them.

• *Strategic planning is often hard and sometimes tedious.* The Leadership Core will be called upon to think hard, to share ideas openly and to commit itself to effective collaboration.

• *Strategic planning is a complex process.* One of the comments we often receive from churches' Leadership Cores during the strategic planning process is that they never expected that they would generate so many ideas. These many ideas will need to be evaluated, revised, edited and agreed upon.

• *The best strategic plans are easy for anyone to understand.* During the strategic planning process the Leadership Core should be encouraged to use simple language and to avoid acronyms and technical expressions.

• *The strategic planning process generates constructive conflict.* As the Leadership Core works together to develop the strategic plan, conflict will inevitably arise as differing views, perceptions and values are expressed. But it is important to point out to the Leadership Core that their differences can be productive and constructive if mutual respect is maintained.

• *Effective strategic planning in the church requires dependence upon God.* If the Leadership Core seeks to develop the strategic plan "in their own power" they will never succeed.

Each member of the Leadership Core will need to commit himself/herself to prayer. But most importantly, each member must also seek to remain broken before God as they allow their personal will to be crushed so that God's will can take its place.

Developing the Plan

As the Leadership Core begins its work on the Strategic Plan, the Mission Statement and Vision Statement are already in place. The task is to develop Strategic Goals, Key Goals and Tasks and Objectives all designed to accomplish the vision that God has given their church. Normally a three year plan is developed.

Perhaps, before reading the description of the planning process below, it would be helpful to look at Appendix I. There you will find "Elements of an Effective Strategy" which gives a basic outline of the planning process and how all the components fit together.

Step One: Strategic Goals.

A good strategy will have three to four strategic goals and no more. Strategic goals are broad goals that identify the major areas of ministry that must be fulfilled in order to reach the vision. Each member of the Leadership Core should prayerfully and individually develop several goals. Then meeting with one or two others will agree on 2 or 3 strategic goals to contribute to the larger group. Finally, the entire Leadership Core will discuss the 7-8 possible strategic goals which have been submitted. These must be narrowed to three or four. There may be feelings of frustration at this point as many ideas will have been expressed and many points of view put forth. As stated earlier, "complexity precedes simplicity." As the team wrestles through this complexity, the strategic goals which will be developed will be stronger and richer. An example of a Strategic Goal is "To develop a church culture that encourages and enables people to give themselves away to bring life to the world." (The examples which are used in this book were developed by the West Shore Evangelical Free Church, Mechanicsburg, PA. Their entire plan, "West Shore Evangelical Free Church - Strategic Plan" is found in Appendix II.)

Step Two: Key Goals.

Key goals are developed next. A good strategy will have three to four "key goals" for every strategic goal. The key goals identify the ministries which will have to be put in place to achieve the strategic goals. The key goals provide the framework for developing the objectives and tasks which flow from them. The Leadership Core develops key goals in the same manner as the strategic goals. An example of a Key Goal is: "To develop and institute an ongoing church-planting strategy."

Step Three: Elder Review.

At this point in the process the Strategic Goals and Key Goals are brought to the elders for their review, input and   approval before moving forward.

Step Four: Objectives and Tasks.

Each key goal will have objectives and tasks which are the "nuts and bolts" of the plan. Rather than providing the direction and framework of the plan as do Strategic Goals and Key Goals, the objectives identify the actual work to be accomplished and the tasks focus on the specific actions required to achieve each objective. Each objective and task must be what is called SMART:

Specific – each statement is complete and clear.

Measurable – each statement contains results that can be tracked and measured.

Attainable – each statement is realistic.

Relevant – each statement helps fulfill the vision.

Time Bound – each statement has a completion date.

Rather than have the entire Leadership Core work on the objectives and tasks, sub-groups are created to develop them. Each sub-group's completed objectives and tasks are sent to the facilitator who reviews and compiles them. They are then sent to the entire Leadership Core for their information. Unless there is a glaring issue, the Leadership Core does not make changes to the objectives and tasks. However, one very important aspect that must be carefully worked on and changes made is the three year calendar. All the objectives and tasks submitted by the various sub-groups will have completion dates associated with them. It will be necessary to prioritize and adjust these so that the most important objectives and tasks are completed first and that all the work is spread out over the entire three year period.

An example of an objective and tasks is:

Objective: "To plant an initial church as a model for ongoing church planting by Jan. 1, 2011."

Task: "Identify a core church planting team by June 20, 2009."

Task: "Have the core planting team participate in specific church planting training by Jan. 31, 2010."

Task: "Have the team assemble project plan with time table, steps and location by June 30, 2010."

Step Five: Elder Approval.

The final Strategic Plan is submitted to the elders for their review to see if there are any major problems or anything missing. If needed, the plan will be sent back to the Leadership Core for any necessary changes. When the elders sign off, the plan is ready for implementation.

Communicating the Plan

After completing the plan, it is important to communicate it to the entire congregation. They have been praying for the process and are anticipating what God has for their church in the coming three years. There are many ways to communicate the plan – a special service dedicated to sharing it; a dessert meeting, a congregational meeting, etc. It is a time to celebrate, to cast vision, and to bring people on board. The Strategic Goals and Key Goals can be distributed to each person and the full planning document made available to anyone who would like to see all the details.

Implementing the Plan

There are several crucial leadership roles that need to be assigned to ensure a successful completion of the plan. There must be a director of the strategic plan; someone who brings together a team to carry it out and holds team members accountable for completion of the goals by the assigned dates. This director is accountable to the senior pastor who is accountable to the elders. Members of the implementation team include individuals assigned to be responsible for each of the Strategic Goals. Their responsibility includes helping provide necessary resources, monitoring results and encouraging workers. These workers may be part of existing ministries or belong to a task force put together to achieve a specific goal.

Final thought

This planning model works for churches of all sizes. We have personally facilitated the process with churches ranging in size from 35 to 2500 adult attendees. The major adaptation, however, is to reduce the number of Strategic Goals, Key Goals, and Objectives and Tasks. It is easy to write large numbers of goals and objectives but almost impossible to implement them if it is a smaller congregation. For a plan to be successful, it must fit the size of the congregation.

Conclusion

We have had the privilege of leading numbers of churches through the process of discerning God's vision for their church and helping them develop a strategic plan. Our interaction with them, from their initial inquiry to the completed plan, has usually involved a minimum period of a year. During this time we have been blessed to get to know pastors, church leaders and members of congregations in depth in a way that otherwise would not have been possible. And we have taken away some lasting impressions from those relationships.

We worked with pastors who were committed to their congregations and had a strong desire to reach their communities. Their schedules were filled with sermon preparation, discipleship, counseling, visitation, and much more. And many felt the extra pressure from the expectation that they were also to be visionary, transformational leaders. It has been a relief to these Godly servants to engage in a process where it was their role to discern, not create, the vision for their churches. They also received valuable input from their leadership communities and had their congregations praying for them. They knew that they were not alone in the process. It was also very helpful for them to have a strategic plan in hand to guide their ministry decision making for several years rather than to constantly be asking, "what is next?"

Elders felt the weight of providing direction and planning for their churches. Many believed that it was their role to do the actual planning themselves. However, by involving other leaders to do the hands-on work, they were drawing on the expertise of those serving in the actual ministry areas. Since they had the final approval of the plan, they were reassured that they fulfilled their Biblical role as elder. They were also gratified with the increased number of other leaders involved with the future direction of the church.

The Leadership Communities, the leaders of all the ministries in the church and everyone who fulfilled a teaching ministry, were very appreciative for the opportunity to provide input to the Senior Pastor prior to his going on retreat to discern God's direction for their church. These committed people really had the pulse of their churches. They thought about and prayed for their churches and had many ideas and suggestions. There was no question that they were greatly looking forward to being part of their churches' future ministry direction.

Each Leadership Core, those who developed the strategic plan, gave 100% to the process. Many were not sure initially what the process entailed, but quickly became immersed and provided excellent and creative proposals. They worked through different ideas with grace and resolve in order to produce a plan that would move the church forward to accomplish its vision. They developed a great sense of team with a common purpose.

Congregations were kept informed so that they could pray with focus. While not intimately involved with the planning process, there was still anticipation on their part to know what the future would look like. Interest in the ministry of the churches was stirred.

Finally, there was one group, the community outside the church that had no idea that the process was going on. But in the long term, they may be the ones impacted the most. Each church we worked with had as a major focus a commitment to engage their local community in order to share the love of Christ. Each church's approach was different, but each church was very intentional in how it was going to move out beyond its walls.

We pray that the contents of this book have provided you with insight into discerning God's vision for your church and developing the plan to accomplish the vision. It is our hope that you approach the process we have described with great anticipation and confidence. And it is our prayer that what we have written will be used in a small way by our Lord to help churches develop their ministries to make an even greater impact for Christ in their communities.

Bibliography

Malphurs, Aubrey. *Advanced Strategic Planning: a New Model for Church and Ministry Leaders* (Grand Rapids, Michigan: Baker Books, 1999)

Appendix I
Elements of an Effective Strategy

VISION STATEMENT:

MISSION STATEMENT:

I. Strategic Goal No. 1: 1 – 3 Sentence Description

    a. Key Goal 1:

        i. task/objective 1:

        ii. task/objective 2:

        iii. task/objective 3:

    b. Key Goal 2:

        i. task/objective 1:

ii. task/objective 2:

iii. task/objective 3:

c. Key Goal 3:

i. task/objective 1:

ii. task/objective 2:

iii. task/objective 3:

II. Strategic Goal No. 2: 1 – 3 Sentence Description

a. Key Goal 4:

i. task/objective 1:

ii. task/objective 2:

iii. task/objective 3:

b. Key Goal 5:

   i. task/objective 1:

   ii. task/objective 2:

   iii. task/objective 3:

c. Key Goal 6:

   i. task/objective 1:

   ii. task/objective 2:

   iii. task/objective 3:

III. Strategic Goal No. 3: 1 – 3 Sentence Description

    a. Key Goal 7:

        i. task/objective 1:

        ii. task/objective 2:

        iii. task/objective 3:

    b. Key Goal 8:

        i. task/objective 1:

        ii. task/objective 2:

        iii. task/objective 3:

    c. Key Goal 9:

i. task/objective 1:

ii. task/objective 2:

iii. task/objective 3:

Appendix II
West Shore Evangelical Free Church Strategic Plan
August 18, 2006

MISSION STATEMENT
Becoming Like Jesus – Head, Heart, Hands, Knees and Feet

Head (Word and Worship)
Heart (Community)
Hands (Service)
Knees (Prayer)
Feet (Missions and Outreach)

VISION
Becoming a church that flows deep and wide into the world

CORE VALUES
Passion for God's Glory
Devotion to God's Truth
Pursuit of Excellence
Loving Relationships
Joyful Service
Mutual Accountability
Humility
Authenticity
Integrity
Equality?

Seeking the Pillar of Fire

GOALS

Strategic Goal No. 1: To cultivate a learning church culture committed to helping each other become more like Jesus.

Key Goal No. 1: To continue the policy of having each ministry in the church set goals for that ministry that help people become like Jesus (head, heart, hands, knees and feet).

Key Goal No. 2: To have 50% of the leadership community of the church partnering in ministry with an apprentice leader by September 2008

Objective 1: To complete a formal leadership apprenticeship program that will be repeated annually from September through May.

Task 1: Identify a leadership development team to implement the tasks described by 10/31/06.

Task 2: Identify qualified leaders within Leadership Community who will train apprentices by Jan. 31, 2007.

Task 3: Communicate the importance of apprentices to qualified leaders by March 1, 2007.

Task 4: Provide training for qualified leaders on how to successfully train apprentices by March 31, 2007 and repeated by March 31, 2008.

Task 5: Have qualified leaders identify their apprentices by May 31, 2007 and repeated the process by April 30, 2008.

Task 6: Provide description of apprenticeship program to potential apprentices by June 30, 2007 and repeated by

May 31, 2008.

Task 7: Begin the formal leadership apprentice process in which apprentices use and develop their ministry gifts under the supervision of a qualified leader by September 30, 2008 through May 30, 2009.

Task 8: Have at least three meetings by Oct. 30, 2007; by Feb. 28, 2008; April 30, 2008 with all of the qualified leaders in one group and all of the apprentices in another to assess and evaluate the effectiveness of the program and to improve it.

Task 9: Officially graduate apprentices to leaders at the Oct. 15, 2008 Leadership Community Meeting.

Task 10. Duplicate tasks d,e,f,g for the 2008-2009 ministry year.

Key Goal No. 3: To create multiple learning opportunities that motivate and enable people to become more like Jesus.

Objective No. 1: To develop an 8-session "Becoming Like Jesus" curriculum that can be used by any adult ministry group in any church by Oct. 31, 2007.

Task No. 1: Develop a curriculum-writing team of 3 people (one SLT member and two other staff members) by October 31, 2006.

Task No. 2: The curriculum-writing team will search for a useful curriculum format by reviewing other training/teaching curricula on the market by January 31, 2007.

Task No. 3: The curriculum-writing team will write/develop an initial "Becoming Like Jesus" curriculum proposal by June 30, 2007.

Task No. 4: The initial "Becoming Like Jesus" curriculum proposal will be reviewed, amended and approved by the staff by August 31, 2007.

Task No. 5: The approved "Becoming Like Jesus" curriculum will be advertised, promoted and made available to all adult ministries on October 1, 2007.

Objective No. 2: To create a six-month "Becoming Like Jesus Discipleship Groups" small group program for those seeking to enter more deeply into the life of the church by Feb. 28, 2006.

Task No. 6: Create a "Becoming Like Jesus Discipleship Groups" leadership team to lead the process by June 30, 2007.

Task No. 7: The team will recruit an initial squad of 7-10 leaders who will be willing to lead the six-month "Becoming Like Jesus Discipleship Groups" by Nov. 30, 2007.

Task No. 8: The team will develop and adapt the "Becoming Like Jesus" curriculum in Objective 1 above to meet the needs of the "Becoming Like Jesus Discipleship Groups" effort by Dec.1, 2007.

Task No. 9: The "Becoming Like Jesus Discipleship Groups" will be advertised and promoted within the church by Jan. 31, 2008.

Task No. 10: "The Becoming Like Jesus Discipleship Groups" will begin meeting by Feb.15, 2008.

Strategic Goal No. 2: To develop a church culture that encourages and enables people to give themselves away to bring life to the world.

Key Goal No. 4: To develop a comprehensive strategy for global and local Missions by May 31, 2007.

Objective No. 1: Hire a Missions Pastor by Dec. 31, 2007 who will be assigned the task of developing this strategy.

Key Goal No. 5: To develop and institute an ongoing church-planting strategy.

Objective 1: To create philosophy/strategy of Church Planting by May 31, 2007.

Task 1: Establish an ongoing prayer team for church plant by 8/1/06

Task 2: Have a staff subcommittee recruit a team of staff, elders, and congregation (total of no more than 8) by Oct. 31,2006 that will lead the effort of developing a clear philosophy and strategy for church planting.

Task 3: Have the church planting team above identify available church planting resources and participate in EDA and other church planting training (by Nov. 30, 2006)

Task 4: Have the team craft the philosophy, strategy, and potential locations by Feb. 28, 2007.

Task 5: Have the team secure approval of the church plant philosophy and strategy with the staff and elders by May 31, 2007.

Task 6: Have the team present the philosophy/strategy to the congregation for information at the Annual Congregational Meeting by June 30, 2007.

Objective 2: To plant an initial church as a model for ongoing church planting by Jan. 1, 2009

Task 7: Identify core church planting team by June 30, 2007.

Task 8: Have the core planting team participate in specific church planting training by Jan. 31, 2008.
.

Task 9: Have the team assemble project plan with time table, steps, and location by June 30, 2008.

Task 10: Have the team prepare a 1-2 year church plant budget by June 30, 2008.

Task 11: Enlist and employ volunteers to regularly assist with church planting beginning June 30, 2008.

Task 12: Begin meeting as a church by Jan. 1, 2009.

Key Goal No. 6: To repeatedly express in verbal and non-verbal forms the vision and value of giving ourselves away to bring life to the world.

Objective No. 1: To form a creative arts leadership team by October 31, 2006 to express this vision by commissioning, creating and supporting "life-giving" art in the church facility and grounds.

Task 1: Form a creative leadership team by August, 2006

to refine and implement the following tasks.

Task 2: Purchase or commission the creation of life-giving art to include, but not be limited to, the following projects:

a. Sanctuary furniture: candelabra, pulpit and communion table, to be completed by August 31, 2007;

b. Lobby and/or sanctuary banners, completed by August 31, 2007

c. Rounded wall across from the nursery, by August 31,2008

d. Framed art throughout the church (3 pieces per year) beginning January 1, 2007;

e. Sunday morning video screen images, by January 31,2007.

Task 3: Commission the creation of life-giving fountains in two or more of the following places, by August 31, 2008: the main lobby, preferably using the marble wall; the field outside the main lobby; the garden above the upper parking lot; the prayer chapel.

Task 4: Redesign and build a missions display, incorporating water of life imagery, to be completed by August 31, 2007.

Task 5: Host a "Festival of Life" art exhibit by March 31, 2007, coordinated with a "Life-Giving Saturday" in which all the ministries of West Shore develop work projects to serve the surrounding community.

Task 6: Launch a "Life Memorial" ministry by January 31, 2008 to solicit memorial contributions to create life-giving gardens along the walking path.

Objective No. 2: To express this vision in verbal form through a sermon series on the Life of Jesus, beginning December 2006 and through the sharing of stories of life during one Sunday service a month.

> Task 7: Create and place "Life-Giving" Scripture signs in the parking lot by April 30, 2007 and along the walking path by April 30, 2008.

> Task 8: Tell "Stories of Life" in at least one Sunday service a month and four sharing services every year, beginning September, 2006.

> Task 9: Launch a sermon series on the Life of Jesus by December 1, 2006, highlighting Jesus' heart for the lost. Coordinate this with the "Festival of Life" in the Spring of 2007.

> Task 10: Ask every major ministry to teach a series focused on bringing God's life to the world in coordination with Phil's sermons and the "Festival of Life" by Nov. 30, 2007.

Key Goal No. 7: To develop and communicate enough opportunities to enable 50% of the church's people to participate in an outreach ministry by Dec. 31, 2009.

> Objective 1: Develop an outreach ministry team that will identify and create outreach ministry opportunities that increase by 50% annually from Jan. 31, 2007 to May 31, 2009.

> Task 1: Recruit the team comprising staff, elders and congregation (total of no more than 7) by October 31, 2006.

> Task 2: Cultivate existing and new relationships with local outreach oriented ministries and churches for the purpose of creating new opportunities for our people, beginning Nov. 1, 2006.

Task 3: Identify current outreach ministry opportunities, differentiating them by level of involvement and frequency of participation by April 30, 2007.

Task 4: Develop and implement a process (e.g. focus groups) to create new ministries and to cultivate additional outreach opportunities within existing ministries beginning May 1, 2007.

Objective 2: Begin holding "Festivals of Life" by March 31, 2007.

Task 5: Create an annual "Festival of Life" designed to communicate the importance of bringing God's life to the world and promoting opportunities to become involved in outreach ministry by March 31, 2007.

Task 6: Create an event within the "Festival of Life" (e.g. "Life Giving Saturday") in which all the ministries of WSEFC develop work projects to serve the surrounding community by March 31, 2007.

Objective 3: Create an effective system and process for communicating outreach ministry opportunities throughout the church utilizing multiple venues and media by June 30, 2007.

Task 7: Develop a system for communicating opportunities via existing print media (e.g. Free Notes and Free Exchange), the Sunday PowerPoint and the website) by June 30, 2007.

Task 8: Incorporate the communication of outreach ministry opportunities into the Connections and New Member classes by June 30, 2007.

Key Goal 8: to cultivate a generous church in which people are challenged and encouraged to be biblical stewards of their resources.

Objective 1: To challenge and encourage elders, staff and the leadership community to model biblical stewardship.

Objective 2: To give 20% of total church income to ministries and missions beyond the walls of our church by 2010 (i.e. approximately $1 million).

Objective 3: Implement a comprehensive stewardship development program that includes annual teaching from the pulpit, in seminars, in fellowship groups, in small groups and in personal financial counseling.

Strategic Goal No. 3: To be a growing church that enfolds people into the life of the body.

Key Goal No. 9: To seek to grow annual attendance by at least 15% over the next 3 years.

Objective 1: Develop ministry programming that will enable 900 new people to attend worship services within three years (by Sept. 1, 2006).

Task 1: Begin a third worship service (with children's ministry) no later than Sept. 1, 2008.

Task 2: Achieve a 50/50 attendance balance in worship services and a 40/60 balance in children's ministry by Sept. 1, 2008..

Objective 2: To launch one growth engines' each year designed to reach and draw new people.

Task 3: Launch a 'New Beginnings' ministry by September 17, 2006.

Task 4: Launch a Sport's Ministry by September 30, 2006.

Task 5: Launch a ministry to the next generation of young adults by Sept. 30, 2007.

Task 6: Launch a ministry to older single adults by Sept. 30, 2007.

Objective 3: Develop and implement a public communication strategy, linked to the three growth seasons (Fall, Christmas, Easter), that will help our people invite friends and family to our church by Sept. 30, 2006..

Objective 4: Maintain 15% annual growth in children and youth ministries.

Objective 5: Secure adequate facilities to enable 15% annual growth.

Task 7: Complete Maintenance Pad and move all trailers, vehicles, equipment and supplies off parking lot by Aug. 1, 2007.

Task 8: Complete Stumpstown Road entrance/exit by March 31, 2008.

Task 9: Secure additional elementary classroom space no later than Sept. 1, 2008.

Key Goal No. 10: To enable 60% of registered attendees to be active in both community and service by fall of 2009

Objective 1: To enable 60% of registered attendees to be active in community by Dec. 31, 2009 primarily through a new and expanded emphasis on small group ministry.

Task 1: Recruit and assemble a "community leadership team" that serves to promote and connect every church member and regular attendee into church community (September 2006).

Task 2: Define the vision and the mission of the small group ministry and how it fits into the overall community strategy of the church (by Dec. 31, 2006).

Task 3: To make participation in community an essential expectation by developing a communication strategy in cooperation with the SLT by April 30, 2007.

Task 4: Launching a "church wide" campaign that shows people the importance of community and increases the number of small groups by Sept. 30, 2007.

Task 5: Organize and implement four social events annually to facilitate the starting of relationships and to move people into greater community. By April 30, 2007.

Task 6: Develop an attendee questionnaire that will enable "Connection Partners" or Small group coaches to connect people into small groups, fellowship groups, and community (September 2006).

Task 7: Create a small group (community) infrastructure to provide support to leaders through coaching and care (by

April 30, 2007).

Objective 2: To enable 60% of registered attendees to be active in service by September 30, 2009 primarily by implementing a church-wide "Ministry by Design" program and an annual ministry fair.

Task 8: Design and implement a program [*Ministry By Design*] that complements the assimilation process by instructing and inviting attendees into gift-based ministry by Sept. 1, 2007 by completing the following:

a. Create a leadership team to facilitate the process (by October 31, 2006).

b. Develop/select a curriculum to enable attendees to discern their God-created design (by Dec. 31, 2006).

c. Develop/select and implement a database of ministry opportunities both in and outside the church (by April 30, 2007)

d. Recruit and train counselors to align attendees with service opportunities (May 31, 2007).

e. Take a "trial" group through the program (by June 30, 2007)).

f. Offer *Ministry By Design* through a variety of venues (by Sept. 15, 2007).

Task 9: Organize a ministry fair(s) that communicates the array of opportunities to the body by April 30, 2008.

Task 10: To make participation in service an essential expectation by developing a communication strategy in cooperation with the SLT by April 30, 2007.

Task 11: Develop a web-based format to inform attendees of ministry opportunities and to provide the means to pursue them by August 31, 2007.

Seeking the Pillar of Fire

Key Goal No. 11: To help 30% of visitors who are looking for a church home to continue attending 12 months after their first visit.

Objective No. 1: Increase our effectiveness in identifying and tracking visitors to our church.

Task 1: Develop and implement methods for more effectively Collecting visitor information (by Nov. 30, 2006).

Task 2: Contact each visitor three times within the first 90 days of visiting the church. Send a letter within the first seven days (by Sept. 1, 2006).

Task 3: Purchase neighborhood mapping software (by Oct. 31, 2006).

Task 4: Identify and implement an automated tracking (computer) system (beginning December 30, 2006).

Objective No. 2: Enfold 30% of our visitors by connecting them in meaningful relationships in the church.

Task 5: Recruit, train, and empower a staff of connection partners to actively connect with all visitors through phone calls, meetings and activities to establish meaningful relationships by Dec. 31, 2006.

Task 6: Develop and implement a follow-up survey to identify and respond to needs and concerns of newcomers by Feb. 28, 2007).

Task 7: Utilize neighborhood mapping information to connect and introduce church members and newcomers through neighborhood events (beginning Jan. 1, 2007).

Task 8: Develop a process where members invite visitors to a small group or fellowship group within the first three months by Sept. 30, 2007.

Task 9: Define and implement affinity groups to connect newcomers by August 31, 2007.

Strategic Goal No. 4: To serve other churches and ministries by helping them develop learning, life-giving cultures.

Task 1: Have our ministry leaders available to meet and discuss with other ministry leaders outside our church when these leaders make such a request (beginning immediately).

Task 2: When deemed useful by the SLT and the staff, have our ministry leaders available to lead training seminars/conferences for ministry leaders outside our church if such a demand exists (beginning immediately).

APPENDIX

Clarifying Definitions for Key Goal 7

"Outreach ministry"—service in Christ's name that focuses on redemptively loving and supporting persons outside of our body with a view toward bringing them to salvation.

"Our people"—refers to adult registered attendees

"Outreach ministry opportunity"—will provide an opportunity to interact with non-Christians and/or provide benefit in support of an outreach ministry.

Assumptions for Key Goal 9

Spring 2006: 1750 (1675 in sanctuary); 2200 @ Easter.

Spring 2007: 2012 (1900 in sanctuary); 2530 @ Easter.

Spring 2008: 2314 (2200 in sanctuary); 2909 @ Easter.

Spring 2009: 2661 (2500 in sanctuary); 3346 @ Easter.

Assumption for Key Goal 10

Participation in community is defined as: Participation in any adult group that provides opportunity for fellowship and spiritual growth.